His
Majesty's
Headhunters

Celebrating 35 Years of
Penguin Random House India

ADVANCE PRAISE FOR THE BOOK

'*His Majesty's Headhunters* is a superb account of the profound and lasting impact of the Second World War on north-eastern India. But more importantly, the book brilliantly unpacks the making and unmaking of British colonialism in the Naga Hills. It is a great and enjoyable read!'— Arupjyoti Saikia, professor of history, IIT Guwahati, and author of *The Quest for Modern Assam: A History, 1942–2000*

'When Mmhonlümo Kikon quotes Simonides at the start, rather than the famous Edmonds epitaph from the Kohima War Cemetery, one knows this is a book with a difference. It is a fascinating and well-researched account of the Kohima siege, divided into preliminaries and the actual battle, one that altered the region's history. Many common beliefs are shattered and, as befits a poet, not only is the account engagingly written, it is sometimes lyrical. All too often, people from other parts of India don't know enough about the region and its history. Kikon has produced a book that is an eye-opener'— Bibek Debroy, chairman, Economic Advisory Council to the Prime Minister of India

'The incredible story of a unique town straddling India's north-eastern horizon, which was witness to an epic battle that secured the destiny of the free world. A spectacular and insightful read'—Nirupama Menon Rao, former foreign secretary of India, and former ambassador to the United States, China and Sri Lanka

His Majesty's Headhunters

THE SIEGE OF KOHIMA THAT SHAPED WORLD HISTORY

MMHONLÜMO KIKON

VINTAGE
An imprint of Penguin Random House

VINTAGE

USA | Canada | UK | Ireland | Australia
New Zealand | India | South Africa | China | Singapore

Vintage is part of the Penguin Random House group of companies
whose addresses can be found at global.penguinrandomhouse.com

Published by Penguin Random House India Pvt. Ltd
4th Floor, Capital Tower 1, MG Road,
Gurugram 122 002, Haryana, India

First published in Vintage by Penguin Random House India 2023

Copyright © Mmhonlümo Kikon 2023

10 9 8 7 6 5 4 3 2

ISBN 9780670096831

Typeset in Adobe Caslon Pro by MAP Systems, Bengaluru, India
Printed at Replika Press Pvt. Ltd, India

www.penguin.co.in

For the three musketeers, Noyingroni, Lumchilo and Rabon;
and for Paomipem Phazang

'When you go home, tell them of us and say
For your tomorrow we gave our today.'
—Simonides, Greek poet

*'Apau puo medo zha ghüterhü
Rükra themvü mevi lar pengutuo.'*
(Youngest son with a big vision, went to war.
Transformed into a star, he will return and
manifest himself.)
—Written by the mother of
Sepoy Saliezu Angami of the
Assam Regiment on his epitaph at the
Kohima War Cemetery

'We'd forgive most things if we knew the facts.'
—Graham Greene,
The Heart of the Matter

Contents

Introduction

How Kohima, as an Administrative Headquarters, Propelled the Nagas to Save Britain

Ensconced in the bosom of Japfu Peak, the imposing second-highest peak in Nagaland, and over what was once a nondescript ridge—more significant as a symbolic seat of the British Empire, its political headquarters to check the incessant raids over the plains as it were—lies Kohima, at the cusp of an unlikely history which never seems to end. From being a forest belonging to an Angami[1] village, which sometimes was left fallow and where jhum cultivation resumed after a cycle, Kohima was a picturesque sleepy slope on a hill. Neither the present-day Nagas nor the mighty colonial powers could have imagined that Kohima would become the site of the most ferocious battle in the annals of human history. It was here that the Allied forces stopped an invading army of the Japanese emperor Hirohito which saved a king[2] faraway in England.

The Battle of Kohima during the Second World War has been written about with momentous vigour and skill by both American and British historians. These works largely attempt to glorify either General Stillwell or Field Marshal the Viscount Slim, or at times simply document the war which won the Allied forces a decisive victory over Japan's expansionist military plan. The victory restored[3] some of what was lost after the humiliation of the attack on Pearl Harbor in 1941 while effectively thwarting the Japanese attempt to expand into the Indian subcontinent[4]. This was not the World War theatre of Europe or the Middle East, and little would the Allied forces know that they were about to shape world history at the hitherto unknown site called Kohima. History, therefore, was told by the victors about a place where mighty Britain retained control even as her significance was on the wane globally.

In a contest organized by the British National Army Museum, United Kingdom, the Battle of Kohima was picked over the more celebrated battles of D-Day and Waterloo, as Britain's greatest battle. The army of Lieutenant General William Slim, consisting of British, Indian, Gurkha and African troops is known to have won the war for the Allied cause in 1944 at Kohima. The combined forces effectively handed a historically significant defeat to the Japanese troops, thereby changing the course of the Second World War[5]. The Battle is often referred to as the 'Stalingrad of the East' by Western scholars and writers. This is already well recorded and the same has been accepted across the world as the authentic narrative.

Historians even say[6] that this was the last real battle of the British Empire and the first battle of the new India. But that is just the tale told till now by everyone except the Nagas. The real (his) story left behind by the Japanese army led by Lieutenant General Renya Mutaguchi and Lt Gen. Sato and the Allied forces led by Slim still largely remains untold and therefore unknown.

Lieutenant General Sato is said to have commented[7] that if it were not for the Nagas, the Allied forces would have been eventually defeated in Kohima, and the Japanese army could have easily secured the Dimapur Railway Station and triumphantly moved towards Bengal via Assam, thus reversing the course of world history. The little that is known about the role the Nagas played in this historic battle is recorded in some books. All one knows is from the records of the valiant officers and soldiers who fought at Kohima. Many writers have managed to cursorily and sporadically mention the help and service rendered by the Nagas while noting the fact that the Japanese Army saw Kohima as the mountain gateway to India. Or perhaps, Japan's ambitious plan considered the Naga territories its western passage[8] to the world in the scheme of military 'spheres of influence'.

Much before it became a battlefield, Kohima was already the political administrative headquarters of the British colonial government since 1878. The story of how Kohima became the capital of the Naga Hills is mired in a unique battle of the colonial forces versus the Angami Nagas. This was one of the first and perhaps the only political administrative headquarters built and finalized for reasons beyond the classic colonial quest for 'Resource and Revenue'. It was an establishment created to partially administer the Nagas as the British were keen on bringing the marauding inhabitants around Khonoma village under control[9].

The frequent raids by the Angami Naga villages in the plains of Dimapur and North Cachar were a nuisance to the British and an irritant for their trading centres. It took forty-six years for the mighty British Empire to establish their political headquarters at Kohima. But it took many more years to secure it. A series of pitched battles later and after hundreds of British soldiers dying at the hands of the warriors, malaria and jaundice, the British were able to secure temporary peace with force and weaponry previously unseen by the headhunting warriors. Why and how did it take forty-six full years for the British to subdue the Angami Nagas and establish their headquarters at Kohima? The story is an exciting tale of war, trade and the bold expeditions of the Angami Nagas into territories controlled by the British like Sylhet and Chittagong in present-day Bangladesh, North Cachar and Dimapur for slave trade, no less, and salt.

The first section of this book will take readers to this period of forty-six years through the lens of important figures and locations. After the Ahoms defeated the Kachari kings in the sixteenth century, the capital city of the Kachari kingdom in Dimapur was abandoned. And the entire area once again was swallowed by thick forests that eventually engulfed the ruins. It was through this route that in the nineteenth century, the first British officers appeared to oversee a suitable road over the Naga Hills to reach Manipur.

Raja Gambhir Singh of Manipur, who had driven the Burmese invaders away from Imphal with the help of the British, was also seeking a similar route through the Naga Hills to reach Dimapur[10]. He had sent several expeditions with the newly acquired guns and ammunition from the British.

This period is particularly important, as the intersection between a global empire and the local intrigues of the various rulers between Bengal and Burma finally led to the creation of a political headquarters for the Nagas. After the Treaty of Yandabo was signed in 1826, the first Anglo–Burmese war came to an end. The peace treaty brought the entire territory of Assam, Manipur, Arakan, Cachar and the adjoining territories under the British Empire. And around the same time, the historical churn in Assam and Manipur tilted towards the total control of the British government without the consent or knowledge of the Ahom kingdom, Kachari kingdom and the others in between.

It also signalled the beginning of the end of Burmese independence. The Burmese also had to pay a colossal sum of one million pounds sterling, crippling the Burmese treasury, and weakening it permanently as the British went on to fight two more wars against the Burmese and won easily against the weakened Burmese king. According to the scholar Joy Pachuau, the Treaty of Yandaboo 'put an end to Burmese claims on the region. It also brought about a political vacuum, as traditional powers of authority in Assam that were already in decline at the time of the Burmese invasion were unable to fill the vacuum caused by the Burmese departure. This provided scope for British imperial expansion into the region, extending eventually to regions beyond the valley.'[11]

The next period is between the establishment of the headquarters and the various skirmishes which gave the final push for the British colonial government to give shape to a policy of excluded areas and partially excluded[12] areas of administration. From 1878 to 1947, the political headquarter took decisions which would change a people practising the animist form of worship into ardent Baptist Christians[13]. The consolidation of their reign through military outreach across the Naga Hills saw various villages transitioning to new forms of administration, with a renewed sense of the common identity dawning in the cauldron called Kohima. And Kohima was not even the name of the place before the British came. The naming and renaming of places and tribes by the British literally altered the history of some communities and locations. The British, in an attempt to identify and familiarize themselves, anglicized a lot of names and gave them names which the natives did not even recognize.

The ridge which the British chose, and around which they built their headquarters, is now a heritage building which has been outsourced by the government of Nagaland as a heritage hotel for guests wanting to have the ultimate colonial experience. Even the famous Khonoma village had a different name. Before the British arrived, it was actually named after a plant called Khwuno in Angami (scientific name being *Gaultheria fragrantissima*). In Tenyidie language, the word is pronounced as Khwunoria, where 'Khwuno' refers to the plant and 'ria' means land. According to one of the villagers I met at Khonoma, the British soldiers started referring to the village as Khonoma as they could not pronounce Khwunoria and the name stuck.[14]

This was the beginning of the entire history of the Second World War in Kohima. In many a conversation, the Nagas cite three reasons for the victory of the Allied forces over the Imperial Japanese Army. First and foremost being the intelligence inputs and the labour service provided by the Naga villagers. Second was the improper planning of the expedition by the Japanese

military and the differences between the plump, bull-headed Lt
Gen. Sato and the inflexible and ruthless Gen. Mutaguchi. The
insubordination of Lt Gen. Sato, who set aside Gen. Mutaguchi's
orders to hold the fort at Kohima and the subsequent retreat by the
31st Division of the Japanese Imperial Army led to the defeat. The
third was the support of the American Air Force in supplying not
only ammunition and rations but also providing air cover which
proved to be the ultimate factor.[15]

Kohima grew from a battlefield of ridges and makeshift
garrisons to the administrative headquarters of the British colonial
deputy commissioner's office, and transformed after India's
Independence into what is now the capital town of the state of
Nagaland in north-eastern India.

That a small place in the Naga Hills would become the
theatre of riveting warfare that led to an imperial victory has
left a legacy often relegated to a bygone era by its citizens but
religiously commemorated by the descendants of both the British
and Japanese soldiers. To trace back the entire trajectory of the war,
the people involved and the range of untold stories would unravel
the sufferings of the people in and around Kohima.

Near Kohima, in a large village called Kigwema, the Japanese
troops arrived as if in alignment with their stars on 4 April
1944 (4.4.44, as the villagers have scribbled with white paint
on a memorial). Why did Lt General Sato of the 31st Division
choose this village as his base? Did they get the support of the
villagers during the Battle of Kohima? A visit to this place conjures
thoughts and images of intrepid forces at war with one another, of
fierce fighting with weapons unheard of by the natives.[16]

How did the founding of a town change the world so much?
Kohima is no longer what it was then. But the dust of history still
lingers on in every sphere of the town, which has now become the
capital of Nagaland, the sixteenth state of independent India.

The naming of the streets, the corners where rice beer is
sold and relished, the memorial of a ravaging war long ago, the

trek atop a hill where the Cross overlooks the city, the sinews and intricacies of every structure, old and new, the story behind it all would take one a longer period to understand. With a resident population of 1,16,870 according to the 2011 census, Kohima is not even the largest city of Nagaland (Kohima district has a population of 2,67,988 according to the 2011 Census. Officially founded only in 1878 as the British headquarters of the then Naga Hills district, it was named as the capital of the new state of Nagaland in December 1963.[17]

Beyond the picturesque tourist brochures promoting the selected attractions of Kohima, there is an unassuming history of memories that a citizen would tell. With the overarching influence of Kohima as a place and also as a centre of power and government in Nagaland, its existence is connected to every nook and corner of the state. Like the catacombs of the ancient world, this colonial era creation contains within its canvas the roots of many cultural and political mobilizations that define modern-day Naga society.

In the following pages, I attempt to trace the journey of each important construct of structure and ideas which embodies the essence of Kohima as a physical homestead and which also seeks to identify the landmarks that define the contours of the melting pot known as Kohima. Right from colonial history till the present day, the affairs of the entire Naga Hills were intricately linked to Kohima. It is not just the town aspiring to be a city on a hill but the multitudinous impact of its reach across Nagaland that informs the idea of Kohima. The haphazard growth of it has been slow-paced and unplanned, and it took decades for a patch of paddy fields to transform itself into a town birthed out of colonial killing fields, with a vibrant, bustling character of its own.

Decoding Kohima is not akin to writing a travel guide but an introduction into a world hitherto known as the site of the greatest battle on earth. From a small café to a heated public discourse on a Tughluqian attempt, from irreverent choir

members to local rockstars, the secret histories of trying to manage
a state to the telling times of hidden gems, you will find the
explosion of ideas upon a culture overshadowing a headhunting
past and an uncertain future. In a predominantly tea-drinking
culture, the invasion of locally grown, roasted and brewed coffee
is something which may not catch the eye of the avid observer as
they write about their encounters in the dark nights of Kohima and
the narrative of violence belying the breezy calm on the surface.

Jane Jacobs, in Greenwich Village, believed that 'Small' was
the future. And Kohima continues to be small and the snail's pace
it has embraced as its urbanization mantra makes it cozy for the
loyal inhabitants as much as its occasional visitors. The history of a
city is not limited to the formation of the town. Kohima is unique
in many ways. It had an accidental birth and the killing fields of
1944 were the site chosen by the British colonial administration
as the headquarters for its attempt to reach out to the warring
tribes rather than to tame them for their continuous exploitation
in the bordering plains of Assam where tea plantations and oil
extractions required protection. The Japanese invasion compelled
the British and Allied armies to settle on a place to stall the march.
This is as much the story of Kohima as it is of the manner in
which this unlikely capital saved the British empire and the Allied
forces from defeat and brought them out from the jaws of death
into an uncertain glory carved into their history books.

Part I

1

Kohima: What's in a Name?

Kohima is the accidental exonym for Kewhima/Kewhira.[18] The British were infamous for mispronouncing the local names and for ascribing spellings to the words they heard, and they were almost always wrong. According to the constitution of Kohima Village, the words Kewhira and Kewhima were used alternatively by the different khels[19] in their narration of the origin of the name of their village. The British name stuck against the indigenous one. Even from the lore available, the place was named by the ancestors as a pristine location where the wildflower Kewhi grows, which attracted many visitors who settled there thereafter. It is a simplified version of what transpired, but the name was derived from the words 'wildflower', 'visit' and 'settlement'.

For the Lotha Nagas, the story goes that the word for present-day Kohima was Khayima[20] and it had a different basis. In the place called Kezhakheno, now in Phek district, where migration stalled for a long period, the Lothas assembled in such large numbers that it exceeded their capacity to enumerate. One of the reasons given by the community is that the huge wave of migration could not be ascertained because the Lotha language did not have a system to count beyond a certain point and enumeration became impossible. Hence it led to confusion in the process of counting. Khayima in Lotha literally means 'lost in count'. Amusing though it may sound now, it was perhaps the case then. They simply did not bother to keep count beyond a certain number, or it was too huge a number to do so. So they left it at that and called the entire process Khayima. The Lothas migrated through Kohima to their present location in Wokha district of Nagaland and remember Kohima as Khayima till date.

The process became a pattern for the empire. What the local communities called themselves or rather the name they knew themselves by was seldom used by the colonizers.

It is not a surprise that the names of many Naga villages or tribes are usually adopted from the mispronunciations of the colonial invaders. Sometimes, it is amazing how a name given to a community or a village becomes the main identity of the present generations. The old becomes unfamiliar and it is never cited, not even in the retelling of history. Some famous villages have simply accepted the names given and there is no quarrel over them. The history of the name becomes a forgotten chapter, and every narration is based on the identity accepted by the present generation.

The entire cosmos of a people changes with the renaming of their villages and tribes, and it is even more difficult to understand the impact of that change when the natives accept that change some 100 years later.

In 1939, when the sub-assistant commissioner at Nowgaon district—which was then charged with the Naga affairs for the British Raj—was sent to investigate the cause for the incessant raids against them, and subsequently punish the great village of Khonoma and also Mezoma in the Angami 'territory' as they then referred to the area, the name they adopted from the neighbours, the Zeliangs, was used without any complexity. The act of naming was simple, touristy and without any design. You ask the first ones you meet who the next-door neighbours are and they usually do not bother much about the veracity or the etymology of the word unless you are writing an ethnographic account. An expedition or a recce would get them in touch with the natives and they would start a conversation about the names or identity of everyone in their vicinity, that is, as far as the eye could see. But true to the Shakespearean dictum, the Nagas duly followed the rhetorical stance of 'what's in a name?'

Thus, it is written by several Angami scholars that the word 'Angami' was coined by the British from the Zeliang word 'Hangamei.'[21] On being asked who their next-door neighbours were, the Zeliang's replied 'Hangamei'. Usually, the source of the information has their own names for their neighbours. And as mentioned earlier, the name given to the next-door neighbour stuck. Scholars usually clubbed the tribes occupying the Barail range with the generic term Tenyimia. However, when the name Angami was given, the restructuring of tribes began according to the various features observed by the administrator–anthropologists who governed the Naga hills. It is ironical to have a term which meant 'robber or thief' hoisted on the Tenyimia living next door by the Zeliangs. This 'derisive' term was used by them to refer to the Khonoma villagers who frequently raided their villages and carried away their livestock and grains and subjugated them to tax and incessant harassment.[22] It is another story that the misnomer stuck to an entire people and it seems as if the British only perpetuated the name by extending it to the majority of the Tenyimia villages. It is clear the Zeliangs did not intend to demonize or give a name to a tribe which would take on a new meaning totally different to the one initially ascribed. The irony is that the term 'kacha–naga', used to refer to the Zeliangs, was given to them by the Tenyimia neighbours, probably from Khonoma when the British asked who their neighbours were. The word used was 'Ketsa', meaning forest, but it was recorded by the British and used extensively in all of their reports as Kacha–Nagas[23].

Let me quote a renowned Naga scholar Dr D. Kuolie[24], who elucidates the above discussion best in his refutation of an opinion piece in the local papers of Nagaland.

The theory of the writer claimed that the term 'Angami' is a corrupted form of 'kerügumia' (thief) from Zeliang language 'kergami'. In fact, the Angami people used it without knowing its source and meaning in the early days. However, during the 1970s, this theory was clarified by the late John of Viswema. According to him, the British army under Captain Jenkin and Lt. Penberton, when about to cross Tenyimia country from Imphal to Assam in 1832, asked the Meiteis, what sort of people lived that side, by pointing at Tenyimia country. They were told 'Ngami' which means 'perfect/independent people'. The word did not conform to the English language and therefore, it was noted as 'Angami'. That interpretation of the late John had a matching version because the velar nasal sound /ŋ/ never occurs in initial English language. To suit to their language, a syllable vowel /a/ was prefixed to the word to form /aŋami/. That version has been accepted by Ura Academy since then. Although 'Angami' is a popular term till today, it has no other meaning in Tenyidie beyond the late John's version. The continuity in use of the term 'Tenyimia/Tengima/Tenyimi' which originates from 'Tenyiu', the name of the forefather of the Tenyimia group, was accepted by all units by their historical knowledge. 'Tenyimia', therefore, means the descendant of Tenyiu. TPO is purely a reunion of the divided family based on blood lineage. Tenyimia or Tenyidie is a canonized term and TPO is not seeking 'Tribal Recognition' from any quarters. The writer's claim, 'Tenyimie consists of a convenient number of Nagaland tribes together with one or more from the outside' is perfectly in line with his earlier writing, 'The Khezamas, the Sopfümas (Mao), the Zeliangs and the Rengmas never hitherto took themselves as 'Tenyimia'. So far to my knowledge, the Tenyimia were in unity-from many a time although irregular, till regular formation established in 1993.

The word Kacha in Assamese means raw, or in this case, pejoratively meant as impure. The classification has to this day evoked a lot of misgivings and it is often used by Nagas to dismiss a Naga tribe on the same basis as it was understood then, causing much heartburn. What was ascribed without any malice was by a strange turn converted into a divisive term by the British. For instance, those who are termed 'Kacha Nagas' among the Naga tribes take offence at being termed as such due to this Assamese definition. One cannot explain the violence of language this demonstrates in the naming and renaming of the people. There are some tribes among the Nagas which have carried forward the debate by revisiting the names given to them. The tribes now want to go back to the names they had for themselves, naturally. But the process for naming them was much easier for the British. There were no debates as to whether they would accept a name given to them or not. Most of them did not even know or bother as much as they do now. The disparate villages belonging to one community did not have a tribal council when the British first came. And so the first people or village to encounter them were the first to either hear of what they were being called or referred to as, and that is how names were adopted inadvertently. The present generation still bears the consequence of a rampant naming spree, as the priority of the colonizers was not to get the names right but resource extraction and revenue collection using violence and excessive force[25].

2

Demon Worshippers

'The Nagas are pure Demon Worshippers and propitiate them by sacrifice in illness or misfortune.'
—S.E. Pearl[26]

The objective was simple. The British had to cut across the Barail mountains, bulldozing through the thick jungles and overpowering whatever resistance they would face from the warriors along the mountain ridges. They had just helped Raja Gambhir Singh establish his rule over the Manipur kingdom by assisting him in chasing away the Burmese invaders.[27] Perhaps it made it easier for their conscience to bear to attack and massacre a 'barbaric' bunch of villagers to construct the route from Dimapur to Imphal via the Naga Hills. The reports were very clear. Reams of papers were filled with words like 'savage', 'headhunters', 'demon worshippers' to describe the Nagas who had repulsed their attack and even managed to kill some of their soldiers using just the spear and the *dao*. These were simple weapons as compared to the firearms the British brought to the battles.[28]

It all began with a road project. It was not the famed silk route but this was equally important for the British. And the

importance of this road was amply illustrated in years to come.
The British had to first find an easy and shorter route to Manipur
for all practical purposes. Be it supplying rations or transporting
their soldiers towards Manipur and thereon to Burma, or to simply
have a channel of communication ready and secure, the road was
necessary. And as for any road construction, a proper survey had
to be conducted. The survey for the road to Imphal through the
Naga Hills started as early as 1832. The survey would have two
different objectives. The language used by the British government
was misleading. The fact that they had no real interest in terms of
resource extraction or revenue collection in the Naga Hills kept
them away from investing any commercial interest in the region.
However, as soon as the route was to be surveyed, they couched
their language in the usual official excuse. 1) The area had been
inaccessible since the Naga tribes around the area were still not
brought under the rule of the British government. 2) Whenever
the British government leaves a certain area out of their benign
attention, it is always because they deigned to exert no influence
over the region for a certain period.

The origin of the special provisions for north-east India can
be linked to the British policy of bifurcating some areas of Assam,
which later became the hill districts of Assam, and four states—
Meghalaya, Mizoram, Nagaland and Arunachal Pradesh (Manipur
and Tripura were princely states; and Sikkim was an independent
country)—in the post-Independence period. Assam, during the
colonial period, had broadly two types of areas—hills and plains.
Finding the cost of administration not being compensated by the
revenue returns, the British found it more expedient not to spend
on running the administration of this region. Besides, the people
from these areas had exhibited strong aversion to the notion of an
outsider ruling over them. Any intrusion, or its apprehension, into
their affairs was met with opposition and hostility. The issues relating
to land, inheritance, forest, dispute resolution, etc., were dealt with
according to the customary laws and through the arbitration of

clan and tribal chiefs. They were declared 'backward areas' under the Government of India Act, 1919. The Government of India Act, 1935 turned them into 'excluded' and 'partially excluded' areas.[29] There was some difference between the 'excluded' and 'partially excluded' areas. The former were not represented in the legislature of Assam, though they were located in the province of Assam. The 'excluded areas' were administered by the governor-in-council under his 'reserved' jurisdiction. In the 'partially excluded' areas, there was some authority of the provincial legislature. Jurisdiction of the courts of British India was limited in such areas. The British followed the policy of minimum interference in the 'excluded' and 'partially excluded' areas. Indeed, there were three such areas in Assam: apart from the two 'excluded' and 'partially excluded' areas, the third excluded area in which the British did not interfere was the tribal area of Assam. The British divided the people of north-east India as belonging to two exclusive areas—plains or hills. The hills were included in the excluded areas.

Facts have now shown that although the way the British colonial government's influence was exerted is couched in administrative language, the years it took to gather that influence were nothing but violent. There is a debate in the colonial official communications[30] about the 'tribal raids and depredations into the nearby plains areas classed as British areas.' What was not mentioned in these reports was that the history of the region had been selectively used while preparing reports to do a survey and later, as it happened, to establish a political and administrative headquarter at Kohima.

After consolidating their rule over Upper Assam in 1828, the British relocated their headquarters to Jorhat from Rangpur. The proximity to the Naga Hills allowed for more interaction. The British knew that the Nagas were interested in salt trade, and in some cases, the capture and exchange of slaves[31]. The Nagas went as far as Sylhet to capture slaves. And when they were not raiding the neighbouring villages for salt or slaves, they would be on the lookout for new guns to purchase. The expeditions by the adventurous Naga warriors always required meticulous planning. Their weaponry being not so much a threat to the Europeans and the Ahoms, they now realized that they would have to devise better stratagems and utilize whatever resources they had to survive the journeys. For instance, raiding another Naga village was relatively easy for the warriors from Khonoma. The challenge was when they ran into the British and their superior firearms.

Establishing Kohima as the permanent administrative headquarters of the British empire in the Naga Hills is beset with untold chapters of bloodshed, gore, violence, and the death of so many brave warriors. In response to the frequent raids by the Angami warriors in North Cachar and the adjoining areas, the British were compelled to give more attention to the raids. The forces required were sent from nearby posts like Halflong. An assessment was made to classify villages as friendly or hostile. Any villagers opposing the advance of the British army were immediately tagged as hostile and action was initiated against them. Should there be some sort of negotiations after the trouncing of a village, it was just to formalize a surrender and exact some form of taxation. It is told in every village now of how the British exacted fines and labour to not only control the village but to exploit their meagre resources. The entire labour force that the British brought along with them was not sufficient and therefore the new labour that they forcefully engaged added to their strength. In this manner they moved from one location to another, traversing the thick and forested precipices of the Naga hills.

The reports[32] submitted by the British officers speak mostly of the wounded and dead soldiers of the British forces but are selective about mentioning the dead and captured Nagas.[33] Their record is replete with hundreds of Nagas being killed and the number of villages destroyed and burnt down. It seems to have been the pattern. Burn the villages and punish the villagers who defied the rule of the British forces. Using their superior firearms, they subjugated one village after the other, till finally, every Naga village was compelled to sue for peace. Villages that did not sue for peace were attacked. When granaries were burnt, it was akin to sentencing the villagers to forced hunger and poverty for the full year till the next harvest. Thus the 'demon worshippers' were ruthlessly plundered and captured whenever they opposed the invasion by the foreign forces. Although the Nagas had maintained a cordial relation thereafter, the stories of the violent defeat were retold over and over again in the villages. And rather than go back to the record of the British officers alone, a foray into the various oral histories that passed down through generations will help us understand the journey of how Kohima emerged as a political hub.

Captain Francis Jenkins and Robert Boilean Pemberton were not just the first survey officers, they also had the sanction to capture and attack any 'hostile' villages.[34] As far as their reports were concerned, they came with preconceived notions about all the different tribes they encountered along the way. 'Sullen', 'clothed in dirt' and 'savage' were descriptions they used generously as they travelled from one village to the next. The search for an alternate and shorter route via the Naga Hills had taken priority over the active pursuit of hostiles. The clearance of the jungles was less dangerous an exercise as compared to the domination of the hostiles.

But before the various expeditions are discussed from the perspective of the Nagas, let us navigate the various hurdles of the British empire's adventurous officers in their quest for a centre at the hilltop.

3

Headhunting in the Genes

'On the question being once put to the Nagas whether they
would like to become the subjects of the Company, they promptly
replied, "No: we could not then cut off the heads of men and
attain renown as warriors, bearing the honourable marks of
our valour on our bodies and faces."'

—John Butler,
A Sketch of Assam, 1847, p. 160

Decapitating with the right blow of the dao, or headhunting, was
the most significant art of warfare practised by the Nagas from the
ancient times right up until 1994.

To win a war was signified by the number of heads the Naga
warriors brought home. Without these heads of the enemies, the
war meant nothing. Headhunting was a source of motivation for
all aspects of life in a Naga village. It gave them vigour and to the
warrior a renewed energy, translating into the virility of crops and
wealth; the warrior with the most heads found stardom and a place
of privilege in the eyes of his villagers.[35]

At first glance, the headhunting practice of the Nagas has
simply been described by its action—savagery of the uncivilized.

It happened at a time when there was no knowledge of guns. And till the British arrived, the Nagas were using the dao and the spear. In present times, it is best to imagine a machete and a javelin, used for chopping firewood or as a sport—all for non-violent purposes. But through stories passed down generations, the agency of oral tradition has brought to light the principles of warfare and the significance attached to the glory and honour of taking off heads in a battle. It is so intrinsic to any discussion on warfare among the Nagas that it is now considered by many to be the keystone of the survival of the race living across the mountainous ranges of Patkai and Saramati.[36] The noted Naga writer, Temsula Ao, reflecting on 'Headhunting' writes, 'In the oral histories of different Naga tribes, the overriding emphasis on head-hunting is that it was a necessary strategy for the survival of each village community. Living in an insulated environment, each tribe began a process of indoctrination that this practice was not only necessary but also good for the people.'

It was more survival than preservation of a race as one village would fight the other through a stratagem of surprise and ambush. The stratagem was always meticulously developed.

There were many reasons for villages to attack each other.[37] Sometimes, when they formed a coalition to attack a bigger village or foe, it was to raid the granary of the bigger village. It was not only an act of vengeance. But, over the years, feuds between villages developed for various causes and vengeance was sought. And this vengeance became the driving force of the warriors. In the brandishing of decapitated heads, the thirst for vengeance was met. It was a celebration, a decisive victory over the enemy, a proclamation of the strength and the prowess of the warrior over the defeated.

Deep within the thirst for[38] the heads was the belief that the soul or the human spirit resides in the head and the act of chopping the enemy's head was like depriving the enemy of the soul too. At least that was the belief that gave them a sense of gratification. The practice of taking heads was not limited to the Nagas alone. However, the practice was considered a rite of passage from childhood to manhood, and it was the key to getting community permission to get married. Among many Naga tribes, no man could get married if he had not taken a head in the battlefield.[39] Such conditions were put in the olden times to ensure that the village ensured a steady flow of warriors and developed a custom so entrenched in the social system that it cemented the practice of headhunting in the community.

'An eye for an eye' was the philosophy[40] when it came to responding to any heads taken from the village by the enemy. In an interesting report by A.J. Moffatt Mills, he writes, 'It is totally incompatible with the Naga honour also to forego taking revenge, and it is incumbent on him to ransom or recover the skull of a relative murdered or captured in war, years may elapse but the murder of a relative is never forgotten and when a favourable opportunity offers probably, twice the number of victims are sacrificed. Retaliation again ensues and consequently there can never be a termination to these exterminating feuds.' Till the killing was avenged by hunting the head of the enemy, the village could not restore its pride.[41] Ferocious and violent as it was, it established the reputation of the warriors as proficient and successful in headhunting. They were not only the role models for all future warriors in the community, but they also became the hunted and therefore needed more warriors to be trained and skilled in the art of warfare for their own protection. The experienced and successful warrior then became the most vicious headhunter in the process—and the taking of his head by an enemy would ensure immediate fame. Vengeance was sought for every head taken and it went on for years and years till the dead were avenged, and the entire village sometimes carried the trauma of not having done justice to the soul thus taken.

Like most headhunting communities in the world, the practice ended with the consolidation of colonial rule in the

Naga Hills. With the permission granted to the missionaries, there were massive mobilizations to dissuade the Nagas from this practice, using the service of the new converts effectively. As late as the early 1990s, there were stray instances of headhunting between some tribes in Nagaland. Covered by the British Broadcasting Corporation[42] (BBC), it attracted global attention, with the anchorperson sensationalizing the news. The practice may have ended but manifestations of the principles of headhunting persist, and that was unduly highlighted in the news media.

In the end, the vivid portrayal of the fierce warriors practising what seems barbaric and yet embodying a culture which preserves a race and a people and the meaning of honour, glory, sacrifice pregnant in the entire process of headhunting ensures that the identity of the headhunters cannot be understood separately from the act. The ritual of[43] seeking a good omen or identifying a bad omen before embarking on any headhunting mission gave birth to the legend of the warrior priest who would not only lead the warriors into battle but be supernaturally gifted enough to predict a victory or a defeat based on data sourced by spies. It was scientific enough to warrant an analysis though. A simple tried-and-tested method became a way of life, a form of practice which reinforced the spirituality of the act and thus assumed religious significance[44].

All these, in essence, defined the warrior who would plan an ambush or a battle and thrive in the wars that he would embark on. It was small scale and yet it had moved the tribes beyond several mountains. It was the pride attached to it that became insignificant in the wave of wars fought to secure their supremacy. It was the artefacts collected later on by the colonial overlords that made the prized possession of the warrior valuable. The entire collection of skulls in a chieftains' residence is a symbol of that pride derived from the expeditions embarked on. To simply be able to buy it or take it as a trophy without having to go through the entire process of headhunting is a trophy of the modern world. Their fascination with this practice ushered in new stories about headhunting.

Some said the headhunters[45] also practised cannibalism. Others found it barbaric enough to call the headhunters savages. Be that as it may, the evolution of communities or tribes who were once headhunters to now Christians reviling their headhunting past as barbaric had to now reconcile with the new realities of Kalashnikovs and Berettas reverberating through politics in the Naga Hills. But it was much before the advent of sophisticated weapons that the headhunters were placed as labourers for the expansion of the empire in the First World War and then as spies, soldiers and labourers again in the Second World War. The tradition waned from expeditions for the village or the tribe to defending their usual trade routes or their raids for salt and dried fish and slaves from the plains of the Dimasa kingdom till up to Sylhet in present-day Bangladesh. With rifles traded or bought from smugglers of the East India Company and deserters of the British Army, especially the Kukis or the subjects of the Manipuri Maharaja, the target of some of the Nagas, especially the Angami Nagas, shifted to the British nuisance in the plains of Chumukedima. For the Naga saw the British presence as an incursion, a nuisance and an unwelcome one at that.

Over the years, the art of warfare for the Nagas remained the same. Any stratagem was limited to winning the battle in the usual guerrilla style. No Sun Tzu or Clausewitz for the Nagas. The attack was mainly an ambush, to startle and surprise the enemy by catching them unawares. 'If ever there was a philosophy of war for the Nagas, it was passed down the generations embedded in their genes', was what many old wise men would say to the younger generations.

4

Headhunted for a Survey

It did not take exactly forty-six years[46] for the British to establish the headquarters at Kohima. For the many who died in the vicious battles, it was a lifetime. For the villages destroyed as a result of the resistance to the British onslaught, it was a millennium. For the brave warriors who attacked the marauding enemies to uphold the honour of the village and their clans, it was the ultimate sacrifice which generations of descendants will laud and remember. Although the first survey party headed by Captain Jenkins and Pemberton started in 1832 from Silchar with the Manipur Levy to begin the series of surveys, it was not until 1878 that a political headquarter was finally established in Kohima for the Naga Hills. As stated, the survey had only one primary objective—to establish effective communication with Manipur. The present-day national highway 29 (NH29) and also the Asian highway 1 (AH1) actually began with this proposed road.

The British colonial expansion was happening on a global scale. The Burmese invaded Assam three times between 1817 and 1826. They marched in waves through the Patkai Mountain ranges, in the present-day Mon district of Nagaland and Tirap and Changlang districts, which are now a part of Arunachal Pradesh. What is significant from this portion of history is the military alignment of the various tribes inhabiting the North-Eastern region. The alliance depended on the current situation and balance of power with the Ahoms or even among the contesting tribes. Later chapters on the battle fought in Kohima during the Second World War will show how unpredictable the reasons were for stitching together an alliance among the Naga tribes. The other route on which the Burmese advanced was through Manipur. Although the Nagas were on both sides of the route which the Burmese took to enter Assam, there was no communication nor contact among the Naga tribes on the southern side—presently in Manipur—and those in the northern parts of Nagaland and the three districts of Arunachal Pradesh. It was only later in the twentieth century that the tribes would meet under the banner of the Naga identity.

Tribes like the Singphos and the Khampti were eager to give as much support as needed to the Burmese in order to establish themselves against both the Ahoms and the British. Their neighbouring tribes, the Wancho and the Tangsa Nagas of Tirap, however, sided with the British to protect themselves from the aggressions of the Burmese Singpho alliance.

When the British finally defeated the Burmese forces (for it was a huge army which came to defeat the Ahoms, and which stayed back to control and rule the Manipuri and Ahom kingdoms), and the infamous Treaty of Yandabo was signed in 1826,[47] the entire region north-east of Rangpur and that which the Burmese had left untouched formally came under the rule of the British empire; even those communities that were not included in the region but were indigenous to the region. Though the war was by no means easy, it was a case of superior supply of ration and reserves that the British could muster which saved them from the possibility of a crushing defeat. The Burmese forces were equally powerful and strong, comprising thousands of elephants and 10,000 troops.[48] They marched through the Naga Hills, not friendly nor an ally to them, where the treacherous terrain and the steep ravines slowed down and weakened the Burmese forces as they descended to the plains to attack the Ahoms. Having defeated them, it was not

easy to keep the region under their control for long. The British
had their allies in every enemy that the Burmese had made. Some
observers now say[49] that if there was an easier route through
Cachar, the Burmese could have easily overrun the British and
the outcome would have been different. The same conclusion was
drawn by many about the Japanese onslaught in the Second World
War. But more about that later.

The Burmese sent a huge force to Manipur in 1819[50] under
Gen. Maha Bandula, the commander-in-chief of the Royal
Burmese Armed Forces. The Burmese march towards Assam and
Manipur was no less expansionist in nature than the British. This
attack led by the great Gen. Bandula was to result in the eventual
downfall of the Ava kingdom itself and is still regarded as the last
defence of the Konbaung dynasty against the British. The general
was also appointed by King Bagyidaw as the governor of Assam
and minister in the court of Ava for his bravery and military
victories. The ultimate objective of the general was not just to
remain in Assam or Manipur but to march on to Chittagong and
Dacca (now Dhaka). He was instrumental in the first Anglo–
Burmese war which ended with the Treaty of Yandabo in 1826.
Bandula is revered as a national hero by the Burmese for his fight
against the British empire. He was a key figure in the Konbaung
dynasty's policy of expansionism in Manipur and Assam. From
1814 till his death in 1825, he conquered Assam and Manipur
and recaptured them again till the Ava had a military garrison of
2000 men at Assam. The British lost no time in planning their
own offensive. They unilaterally declared the Cachar and Jaintia
British protectorates, managing to provoke the kingdom of Ava.
Maha Bandula advocated an offensive against the British, leading
to the first Anglo–Burmese war. This would eventually lead to the
downfall of the Ava kingdom. Compared to the second and third
wars fought between them, the first was a defiant battle put up
by the Burmese under Gen. Bandula against an overwhelmingly
superior force. Gen. Bandula, respected by the British and

Burmese alike, was leading from the front at the battles of Yangon and Danubyu. He advocated the offensive and till his last breath at Danubyu, when British mortars struck him, he was the inspiring force for the Burmese army. He did not live to see the signing of the treaty and would not have liked the outcome.

The British sustained the entire campaign through the abundance of resources at their disposal and also due to their superior weaponry. The only saving grace for the Burmese army was that the casualties were more on the British side than the Burmese.

There was an atmosphere of discord in the Manipur kingdom. There were internecine fights among the princes, which led to conflicts, precipitating the weakening of the kingdom. This was used to their advantage by the Ava kingdom. Maharaja Marjit Singh was in no position to withstand the marauding forces from Burma and had to surrender. The next seven years under Burmese occupation are considered one of the darkest periods in Manipur history. The same fate fell on the Ahoms when the Burmese invaded Assam. Stories of unrestrained loot, rape, inhuman torture abound. The most barbaric atrocities on the civilians were perpetrated by the Burmese army. Gambhir Singh managed to escape to Cachar along with his elder brother Chourjit Singh. There, he slowly grew under the patronage of Maharaja Chandra Gobind, the Cachar king. The motivation to retake their territories was propelled by the untold sufferings of the people at the hands of the Burmese invaders. The prince without a kingdom was now an experienced warrior and a sharp military strategist. He struck a deal with the British army and formed what was then called the Gambhir Singh Levy with over 500 troops—it was later renamed the Manipur Levy.

A combination of strategic alliances with the Ahoms and the Kacharis helped the British push the Burmese back.[51] By then they had already managed to strengthen the Manipuri Maharaja, Gambhir Singh, to strike and overthrow the Burmese in Manipur. The attack on the main supply line of the Burmese army was but a small enactment of what the Japanese army would face in the next century. The theatre of the Second World War was already being charted in this war against the Burmese. Having ended the 600-year rule of the Ahoms, the Burmese were set to use this as leverage against the British even in Mandalay. Things did not go as planned. Rather, the British ended the rule of the Burmese king over the western part with the Treaty of Yandabo once and for all. It is worth mentioning that the Burmese invasion pushed the Ahom royals and nobles to the Naga Hills, particularly in the Konyak, Lotha and Ao region, taking shelter as they had maintained throughout the age-old relations between the Ahoms and the Nagas.

While the Burmese were overthrown from the North-east region, the expectations of both the Ahom princes and Maharaja Gambhir Singh of Manipur were high.[52] The political atmosphere at that time was theirs to exploit. It was Gambhir Singh who had the advantage of rallying his forces as he had gathered the support of the Manipuri princes and the nobles and strategically enlisted the support of the British with the formation of the Manipur Levy. The combined force thereby secured firearms and proper military establishment for Gambhir Singh, who had by then taken over as the Maharaja of Manipur. As far as his actions went, any collaboration with the British was strategic and could not be considered as permanent. The overthrow of the Burmese forces from Manipur made him a hero in the eyes of his people and indeed he was instrumental in the liberation of the Manipuri kingdom from the oppressive rule of the Burmese. Under his iconic leadership, the hope for expansion and further consolidation of the Manipuri kingdom was natural. Once he wrested control of the kingdom, he was also able to secure his hold over the subjects. In the agreement with the British after the Treaty of Yandabo, the Kabaw valley was handed over to the Burmese.[53]

It was only a matter of time before his attention would turn towards expanding his control over the Naga Hills much beyond what his eyes could behold. The Angami 'country', as the Tenyimia region was then simplified, had always held his attention. To the Manipuri king, the hills were inhabited by the Nagas who were known as the Angamis. But people in the villages surrounding the valley were referred to mostly by the names of their village. It was not necessary to club them as a tribe. To the Maharaja, they were not a unified entity. Although the hill people who form part of the Tenyimia family referred to themselves mostly by the name of their village, such a cluster was not recognized by the Maharaja, more out of ignorance of the word then for lack of words to identify them. Besides the territorial expansion of his kingdom, which meant more soldiers and subjects, he would have ready access to Assam and also the rich and tastier rice that the Nagas harvested.

One quick diversion about the rice found in the Naga Hills. H.H. Godwin-Austen, the deputy superintendent of the Great Trigonometrical Survey of India appointed to survey the Naga Hills and Manipur Boundary in 1872, and who was also an explorer and a geologist, had this to say about the rice grown and eaten in the Naga Hills: 'I have never, even in the better cultivated parts of the Himalayas, seen terrace cultivation carried to such perfection, and it gives a peculiarly civilised appearance to the country. The rice raised is exceedingly fine and very nourishing, containing much sugar and gluten; it appears coarse when compared with the table rice of Manipur and Assam, but we always preferred it to the latter, and it can be cleaned to boil quite white. The Naga rice owes its fineness to the natural richness of the decomposed clay shales, but they also manure at the time of breaking up the soil and before the water is let in upon the fields. The rice is sown in nurseries and planted out just before the rains.'[54] It would seem that the taste and feel of the rice in the Naga Hills moved him so much that he was emotionally composing a paean to the rice found there. From Burma to Kashmir to the great Karakoram glaciers and the Kanchenjunga Mountain, he had explored it all for the British government before coming to Bhutan and the Brahmaputra

Valley. With his vast experience, it can only be said that his love
for the Naga rice was special. He dedicated a paragraph of his
report on the survey operations around the Barrail mountains to
the rice grown there. The iconic picture of the green terrace fields
adorning the walls of many a visitor to Nagaland around Kigwema
and Jakhama villages was mentioned by him during this survey.
From his description, anyone would conclude that the rice found
there would itself be something to lead an expedition for.

But before the death of Maharaja Gambhir Singh in 1834,
the explorations of Captains Jenkins and Pemberton in 1832 led
to the attack by Maharaja Gambhir Singh on the Tenyimia areas
in the year 1833.[55] Gambhir Singh's expedition can be called the
second expedition of the British, as the Manipur Levy was led
by Lt Gordon along with Gambhir Singh. The first survey had
proven to the British that it was not going to be an easy ride for
them and that the fighting which they expected to be quick and
swift would take them some years to finally settle. This was much
beyond what they had bargained for. Some of the adventures, for
it was no less an adventure for the British army, show the extent of
their struggle with whom they knew as the fierce warriors of the
Angami Nagas.

5

The Maharaja and His Long-Haired Warriors

'A sculptured stone at Kohima, a carved uplong pillar with a flat stone resting on its base is said to have perpetuated the memory of this incident. The stone was revered by the Manipuris as a divine symbol. The stone has slipped down in a soil erosion lately.'
—Observation by Dr H. Bareh

Kohima is now the city on a hill, a capital of a state engulfed in the sudden mist of clouds when the weather gods love the rush of schoolchildren bustling agog with spurts of laughter and joy. The 'carved uplong pillar' referred to in the quote above is still in existence in Kohima, safely shifted to the Nagaland state museum in Kohima. It has been a tradition of the Manipuri kings to erect stone pillars to commemorate their victories in the past. In fact, the Manipuri Raja Pamheiba is known to have erected a stone pillar in Upper Burma after one such victorious war. For the pillar in Kohima, the feet of Raja Gambhir Singh were engraved in the slab of stone in 1833.

Initially, the stone was placed at Phoolbari in Kohima in a park where visitors thronged more to rest from shopping around town than to see the pillar. It was shifted to its present location

due to the threat from an impending landslide. Over that space
now stands the Oking Hospital, a private healthcare establishment
towering over the city, a landmark in itself. Visitors no longer view
it with much interest as it stands obscurely in one corner of the
museum, which serves as the directorate of the arts and culture of
the government of Nagaland.

It was not so when it was installed in 1833. Gambhir Singh
had always nurtured the ambition of expanding his territory.
And before the advent of the Anglo–Burmese wars led by Gen.
Bandula, the British empire found it convenient to place the
courageous Raja at the heart of their strategy to defend the long
borders with Burma. While he benefitted immensely from the
East India Company's (EIC's) policy, he had great plans to use
the situation to his advantage. A puppet king was not something
he had imagined his future to be. Given the ordeal he had to go
through to reach this stage at the end of the Anglo-Burmese war,
he was not willing to reduce his position to a mere gatekeeper
of the British. Gambhir Singh represented a classic case of
ambitions meeting opportunity. He wanted to drive the weakened
Burmese forces away from Manipur. The EIC officials at Kolkota
wanted to open trade routes till China via the Kabaw Valley and
had to confront the Ava kingdom. The two powerful intentions led
to so many historical changes. The Manipur Levy enabled him to
reclaim his rightful place on the throne of Manipur. And when
his support was required by the EIC, he was more than willing
to extend his help. The expedition to the Naga Hills, whatever
the reasons the EIC may have shared with him, set in motion his
own ambition of not only subduing the surrounding villages in the
Naga Hills but putting a stamp of his authority. He was as astute
as he was brave. The treaty of Yandabo provided him with two
opportunities. Both the Ava and the EIC inadvertently needed his
service. The Burmese did not want a political agent of the EIC to
run the kingdom of Manipur just as much as the EIC considered
Manipur a buffer zone between their jurisdiction and Burma.
They were eyeing the various markets scattered across the path

to the larger Chinese markets and the Ava needed to be brought within their control.

Gambhir Singh did not anticipate then that he would be compelled to give away the Kabaw Valley to the Burmese king.[56] As much as he was a shrewd military leader, he was seen as a liberator by his people from the brutal and harsh occupation of the Burmese Army. But many accounts suggest that his military expeditions found him to be as cruel and harsh upon his enemies even in the hills. For the EIC, they were happy to allow him to penetrate the Naga Hills with his forces as long as he subjugated them for the EIC. Frequent annual raids by the Nagas on the plains could not be contained since the EIC did not have the time to give attention to that nor provide a permanent solution to the raids on their subjects. It was continuously affecting their trade as their subjects were harassed with such ferocity, hampering their economic interests.

In addition to that, the Ava claimed the land till the outskirts of the Manipur kingdom. This annoyed the British to no end.

Gambhir Singh himself was willing to emulate his illustrious ancestor Garib Niwaz and attack the frontiers of the kingdom of Ava. Thousands of Manipuris had already been taken as slaves by the Burmese to Mandalay and it bothered the Maharaja.[57] Given this background to the fate of his kingdom and geopolitical hankering over his rule, Gambhir Singh used it to strengthen his army by recruiting more Manipuris in the Levy. Even when he was told by the British to stop recruiting soldiers to the Manipur Levy, he cited the expeditions as his reason and expanded the Levy to around 2000 soldiers. The cost was burdensome for the British although the mission was necessary. Maintaining the army with enough firearms and supplies was becoming a problem. However, the Governor–General William Bentinck supported the policy of using the Maharaja to secure the borders.[58]

The Kohima stone, as Major General James Johnstone called it, was symbolic of Raja Gambhir Singh's conquest over the Angami Naga Hills. There are old people who still tell tales of long-haired and able-bodied soldiers carrying swords and shields, attacking the villages on their way till Kohima Village. The firearms were at first thought to be sticks by the Naga warriors. When the ball of fire coming from the firearms struck the warriors dead, it was nothing but magical. The fear of sorcery penetrated deep into the psyche of the Naga warriors. For, if there was anything to be wary of, it was the unknown mystery of the evil, a concept they readily understood. Lt Gordon, adjutant of the Manipur Levy, had led the attack along with Gambhir Singh. This arrangement was established right from the formation of the Manipur Levy. Although the recruitment of the soldiers was mainly from the Manipuris, there was a formal overseer from the side of the EIC.

According to James Johnstone, the influence of the Manipuri kingdom over the surrounding areas was on the wane till the Anglo–Burmese war reinvigorated its reach and power. The influence they have had on the hill villages 'fell into abeyance'. And using the Manipur Levy, Gambhir Singh was able to reassert the influence of the Manipur kingdom over the hills. Kohima was the biggest village that he had been able to subdue with his newfound force. Some members of the present-day Kohima village refer to their history and refute the claim of James Johnstone that the entire Kohima village was subdued. In the book *The Angami Nagas*, anthropologist J.H. Hutton goes into details about the conduct of the various khels[59] in matters of war or polity. Kohima was indeed a big village with more than 800 households. In another report by A.W. Davis, in Census of India, 1891 (vol. 1, p. 237 f.) the different khels displayed indifference among themselves. His observation was acute, at least for some part of Naga society. The essence of governance of the Naga village rested on the khels and not the village as a whole. Khels are formed based on either a common ancestry or groupings determined by 'exogamous divisions'. 'Between the khels in the same village great rivalry exists, which in old days used to lead to blood feuds and frequent fighting. Indeed, the inter-khel feuds were and are now practically extinct, but inter-khel feuds are kept alive, and result not infrequently at the great drinking festivals in riots and free fights, in which lives are occasionally lost. I know of no Angami Village of any size which is not divided against itself by bitter feuds which exist between its component parts.'

He produces a very unsavoury account by P.T. Carnegy, then political officer in the Naga Hills, dated 12 September 1876, to substantiate his observations.

'In the middle of July a party of forty men of Mezoma went over to Kohima, and were admitted by one of the Khels friendly to them, living next to the Puchatsuma quarter, into which they passed and killed all they could find, viz., one man, five women, and twenty young children. The people of the other khels made no effort to interfere, but stood looking on . . . one of the on-lookers told me that he never saw such fine sport (i.e., the killing of children), for it was just like killing fowls.'

It is a gruesome account, and anyone will be alarmed now upon reading or hearing the story as part of the report. Perhaps it did not occur as told for there is lack of evidence to substantiate the report. All first-hand reports may have to be taken with a pinch of salt. But it does not refute the insinuations made about the cruelty of the villagers then.

It may have been that the entire Kohima village was not subdued as the other khels had no interest in the fight against Gambhir Singh. His conquest over Kohima is remembered by the villagers even now for the ferocity of the attack and the number of captives taken away to Imphal by the victors. To this day, the thought of some ancestors captured and taken to Imphal invigorates the imagination of the villagers. Where will the descendants be? What would have become of them? In later chapters, we will encounter a similar story with a definitive ending: The descendants of one fugitive reaching out to their ancestral village and their clans long after the British had left and their hideout had become part of Manipur state whereas their ancestral village stayed as a prominent tourist village in Nagaland. But the women who were taken as captives had been married off to the soldiers and the menfolk subsumed into the Meitei society, so much so that it will be difficult to trace their descendants.

The mark of conquest is unique for Kohima. Gambhir Singh secretly nurtured an ambition to rule over most of the hills without any interference from the British or the Burmese. He had established himself on the throne. The year he marched up to Kohima also was the year he ceded the Kabaw Valley to the Burmese in a deal long sealed before his coronation as the Maharaja of Manipur. For 6000 siccas annual payment, the Maharaja accepted the offer proffered by the EIC. This was clearly in line with the agenda of the EIC in ensuring that the territories which could have been occupied by the Manipuri king after a successful conquest were left to the Burmese or the Angami Nagas in exchange for annual taxation as a form of both influence and indirect control.

The cruelty over the Angami villages Gambhir Singh defeated was no less horrifying than the Burmese terror over his own kingdom in what is now remembered as the seven years of devastation. The horror and fear Gambhir Singh instilled in the vanquished during his campaigns are also well-etched in the oral history of many tribes and communities. It was said that during his Kohima campaign, some prisoners of war were also buried alive in front of the public so as to implant terror in the minds of the indomitable Nagas. The sculptured pillar is said to have been erected over the body of a boy buried alive. History based on written documents may not support this claim and dismiss these memories as rumours at best. However, it should be noted that memories based on oral tradition have been given the credibility that they deserve in recent times.

The reason Gambhir Singh embarked on this expedition was to follow the same route used by the survey party. He did not expect the large confederacy of the Angami Nagas which attacked and retaliated against his convoy. Taken by surprise, he responded with a well-armed force and managed to crush the confederacy. Since he did not occupy the villages he defeated, the succeeding years saw constant raids and attacks by the Nagas in the Manipur valley. The raids continued till the establishment of the Naga Hills by the EIC in 1866.

6

The Not-So-Strange Alliances

A short background of what was happening in the kingdom of Manipur around the time the British mounted their various expeditions in the Naga Hills will situate the entire series of events in the context of the Manipuri kings and their priorities.

Gambhir Singh (1788–1834) did much for Manipur during his comparatively short reign. Born Chinglen Nongdrenkhomaba on 5 March 1788 at Langthabal Palace, Canchipur, he died in 1834 at the age of 47.

The territories of Manipur varied according to the mettle of its rulers. Sometimes they held a considerable territory east of the Chindwin river in subjection, and at other times only the Kabaw Valley, a strip of territory, inhabited not by Burmese but by Shans, and lying between the Manipur hills and the Chindwin. Territories captured and lost is part of that chapter of Manipur history which has resonance till today.

The pinnacle of the Manipur kingdom's expansion started with the accession of Pamheiba, also known famously as Raja Garib Niwaz, to the throne of Manipur in 1714. The significant socio-religious transformation came about during his long reign. The spread of the Ramananda sect of Vaishnavism in Manipur began under his reign and patronage. The Vaishnavite missionary Shantidas Goswami came from Sylhet under the then undivided Bengal. Garib Niwaz converted to Vaishnavism and thus began the spread of Vaishnavism among the Meiteis. It was during this time that he ordered the burning of the Puyas, the old religious books written in the now archaic Meitei script. But that was not his only significant contribution. Manipur reached its zenith as an independent military power during his reign. It is difficult to imagine now with the present imbroglio in Myanmar, but his offensives against the Burmese were so successful that he established his supremacy as far as Mandalay. The territorial expansion of Manipur was also the farthest during his reign. The death of Pamheiba or Garib Niwaz signalled the decline of Manipur and the decrease in the territory was in proportion to its increase during his reign.

The Burmese, not forgetting the incursions of Garib Niwaz, launched successive military invasions from 1755 till the Treaty of Yandabo in 1826. The Burmese, under Alompara, invaded Manipur in 1755 and then again in 1758. This invasion was led by Alompara himself and he successfully managed to drive the Manipuri king, Raja Jai Singh (Bhaigyachandra), straight into the arms of the British. The treaty between him and the British was signed in 1762, and the alliance had the explicit agenda of both offensive and defensive purposes. However, the alliance did not hold much water as the Burmese invaded and ransacked Manipur in 1765, and Raja Jai Singh fled to Cachar.

Manipur's relation with the British began in 1762, when Governor Harry Verelst of the Bengal Presidency entered into a treaty with the Raja of Manipur. As this treaty came to nothing, the empire's connection with the 'little' state really dates from 1823.

Between the immediate successor of Garib Niwaz, Raja Jai Singh, and Gambhir Singh, there is a complex thread of backstabbing and takeovers from the various Manipuri princes, a chapter of conspiracy and fratricidal killings, which eventually led to the dethronement of Chaurjit Singh by his brother Marjit Singh with the support of the king of Ava. It came at a price, however. For the support of the Ava, Marjit Singh had to renounce all claims on the Kabaw Valley and announce his allegiance to the king of Ava.

Compared to Manipur, there were three Burmese invasions into Assam from 1817 onwards. The allegiance of Marjit Singh was tested in 1819 when the king of Ava invited Marjit Singh to attend his accession ceremony. The decisions of Marjit Singh, spurred by ambition at the time of his own ascension and now by defiance after he was invited by the king of Ava, had inadvertently brought two notable setbacks for the Manipur kingdom. Dethroning his own brother Chaurjit Singh resulted in ceding the Kabaw Valley to the Burmese. Not attending the ascension ceremony led to one of the cruellest invasions of Manipur by the Burmese. The seven-year devastation period is still remembered as the darkest period in Manipur history. King Marjit Singh had to flee to Cachar.

Besides Heerachandra, a nephew of Marjit Singh, there was no effective rebellion against the Burmese garrison left in Manipur. He led many guerrilla offensives against the Burmese army during their seven-year rule in Manipur, much to the chagrin of the king of Ava. Unable to capture him, distraught at not containing his guerilla warfare, the Burmese were regularly attacked by a small band of loyal warriors led by Heerachandra. Although he could not chase the Burmese away from Manipur, his heroics against the ruthless Burmese forces rattled the Burmese to no end.

It was during this time that the fiercest of all the princes came on to the scene.

After the Burmese invasion in 1819, Manipuris were either driven out or carried off into slavery in Burma. The Manipur royal family were rendered homeless and became fugitives. For the Manipuri prince, the British empire woke up from its slumber seven years too late.

The British frontier was represented by David Scott, agent to the Governor–General.[60] Scott met Gambhir Singh, after which the agent to the Governor–General allowed him to raise 500 men (Manipur Levy), which was later increased to 2000— including cavalry, infantry and artillery. Two English officers, Capt. F. Grant and Lt R.B. Pemberton, were attached to this force of the Manipur Levy.

The Burmese were driven out and Gambhir Singh was recognized as Raja of Manipur, and the Kabaw valley was included within Manipur. Gambhir Singh was allowed to 'rebuild the prosperity' of his little kingdom.

Later, in a unilateral agreement, the Kabaw valley was given to the Burmese for '6000 sicca rupees per annum', and according to James Johnstone, Gambhir Singh accepted it, saying, 'You gave it me and you can take it away. I accept your decree.' The Kabaw valley was handed over to the Burmese on 9 January 1834, and on that fateful day, Gambhir Singh died in Manipur of cholera.

According to Johnstone, Gambhir Singh's orders were always implicitly obeyed and this too was carried into effect. His army then consisted of about 5000 men in eight regiments of infantry and an artillery corp. The famous cavalry was a thing of the past, and many of the infantry were quite unacquainted with the drill. There were eight three-pounder brass guns, and two seven-pounder mountain guns given to them as a reward for services in the Naga Hills, one of which did admirable service in the Burmese war. Most of the infantry were armed with smooth-bore muskets, some being of Enfield Pattern.

Besides the above, there were about 1000 to 1200 Kuki irregulars. A Manipuri military expedition was a strange sight— the men, besides their arms and ammunition, carrying their spare clothes, cooking vessels, food, etc., on their backs. All the same, they could make long and tiring marches day after day on poor fare and without complaint, and at the end of a hard day would build a camp themselves and fortify their position with great skill, however great the hardships they had undergone. It was a standing rule that in an enemy's country, a small force should always stockade itself, and a Manipuri army, well commanded, was then able to hold its own against a sudden attack.

On their return from a successful expedition, the troops were greatly honoured, and the general in command accorded a royal welcome, and it was an interesting sight to see the long thin line of picturesque and often gaily clad troops, regulars and irregulars, winding their way through the streets and groves of the capital, bearing with them spoils and trophies gained in war. Here, a party headed by banners, there some Kukis beating small gongs and chanting in a monotonous tone exemplified the victory march.

Finally, after marching round two sides of the palace, they would enter by the great gate, pass between the Chinese walls, and again between the two lions (Kanglasha), and be received by the Maharaja at the Gate of Triumph. Their general would throw himself at his feet and receive his chief's benediction, the greatest reward that he could have.

According to James Johnstone, about the year 1250, a large Chinese force invaded Manipur and was 'signally defeated'. The Chinese taught the Manipuris silk culture, and a number of them were settled at Susa Rameng in the valley, where they still have their descendants. The Chinese also taught the art of brick-making, and erected two solid blocks of masonry in the palace, between which the road to the Lion Gate passed. These blocks were levelled to the ground by the Burmese invaders but rebuilt on the old foundations by Gambhir Singh.

Gambhir Singh made all the roads in his territory safe, and subdued or sued for peace with the different hill-tribes who were restive during the troubles with Burma. Imphal, the old capital, had not been reoccupied, and a new palace had been built at Langthabal.

The Manipur Levy was maintained till 1835 when the government of India withdrew their connection from it, and ceased to pay the men. During Gambhir Singh's time, the role of the political agents was crucial in maintaining his relations with the British empire. Any attacks on Burma would now have to be within the ambit of British policy. After his death, various political agents witnessed the succession to the throne in Manipur.

Major Grant left Manipur, and Captain Gordon, who had been adjutant since 1827, was made political agent of Manipur. Captain Pemberton had long since been on special survey duty.

Captain Gordon died in December 1844. He was much liked and long remembered by the people whom he had greatly benefited, among other ways by introducing English vegetables and fruits. He was succeeded by Lt (afterwards Colonel) McCulloch.

Raja Nar Singh died in 1850, and was succeeded by his brother Debendro, a weak man, quite unfit for the position. In 1850, young Chandra Kirtee Singh invaded the valley with a body of followers, and Debendro fled Manipur for the Naga Hills.

At this time, the Naga Hills were still under a political officer whose actual jurisdiction was limited to the villages which had paid tribute to Johnstone. He was supposed to exercise a certain influence over many of the large villages, but the influence was lessened by the feeling entertained by the Nagas that their stay in the hills was uncertain, and that for all practical purposes, the Manipuris were the power most to be reckoned with, and from the British point of view, it was very desirable that the headquarters be moved to Kohima.[61]

A dispute with Manipur and the Naga Hills, especially Mezoma village, due chiefly to vacillating conduct, was now going on, but its chiefs would not accept British terms, and an expedition to coerce them was in preparation. Carnegy was a political officer, a man of ability and determination, and very pleasant to deal with. During the dispute with Mezoma, the other villages held aloof, thinking the village was able to hold its own, and waiting to see which side gained the day. At the proposed expedition to Naga Hills (Mezoma), James Johnstone had brought up 100 men of the 35th Native Infantry, from Cachar. He started from Manipur on 3 December 1877, having sent on the 35th a Manipuri force of over 300 men under the minister Balram Singh.

Johnstone's intention was to march on Mezoma by a track which would avoid the powerful villages of Viswema, Kohima, Jotsoma and Khonoma. While all these preparations were on, he received the news that the Manipuri outpost of Kongal Tannah, on the borders of the Kabaw valley, had been attacked on

14 December by a party of men sent by the Raja of Sumjok or Thoungdoot, and eight men killed. The Maharaja begged him to return and he returned on 17 December, leaving the troops in Naga areas, with 'the Nagas being unwilling to submit'. The Nagas were 'making overtures' instead to Maharaja Chandra Kirtee Singh who sternly declined their offers, and threatened that if they did not speedily yield to the British authorities, he would send a large force to aid the British.

'The Naga Hills Campaign of that year had no further interest for Manipur, and it had a sad ending for us,' remarked Johnstone.[62]

The involvement of the British political agents in the affairs of the Naga Hills, as briefly mentioned in the two paragraphs above, demonstrates their increasing participation in the strife between the Nagas and the Valleys of both Manipur and Cachar. It is worth noting that when Gambhir Singh started his campaign in Cachar, it was under the rule of Govinda Chandra. Gambhir Singh and brothers Chourjit Singh and Marjit Singh were accused by Govinda Chandra of dethroning him. Gambhir Singh was later suspected of the assassination of Govind Chandra on 24 April 1830. However, his claim on Cachar was denied by the Treaty of Badarpur and Captain Thomas Fisher of the British empire took charge of Cachar with his headquarters in Cherrapunjee.

7

When Guns Replaced the Spears

Before the guns came blazing with the colonial army in their quest to tame the wild natives, as they saw it, the Nagas had only heard of the new weapon which spewed a ball of fire accompanied by a loud noise, and how it managed to kill a warrior when the fire entered the body. This was a spirit of a different kind, one which they had never seen in their lives nor heard of in their legends. That the bullets were regarded as fire released from a gun was described by a coolie from the Synteng tribe to Lt R.G. Woodthorpe.[63] 'Oo! They think the bullets are fire, and that if they pass through any substance full of moisture the fire is quenched, and the bullet becomes harmless. In the Khasi and Jaintia war, we used to build stockades with plantain stems in this belief.' The above conversation was recorded during an expedition to Wokha district of Nagaland where the British Army officer Robert Gosset Woodthorpe's curiosity was aroused, during the battle with the Lothas, by the strange adoption of covering their shields with 'strips of plantain bark which made them glisten most brightly'. It was ingenious to make such an observation of the deadly and fatal impact that guns would inflict on the Nagas. The Synteng coolie's observation and the similar conclusion of the Khasis and the Jaintias of the new weaponry used by the British army is interesting to note: how the two different communities, no less fierce in war than each other, reacted initially to the bullet and responded based on a similar assumption.

The bemusement of R.G. Woodthorpe over the use of the plantain in the battle for control over Wokha is therefore not just comical but also valuable as it provided him with insight into how the natives strategized for any battle. In his general report, Woodthorpe, who at that time was a lieutenant in the British Army had initially been commissioned in the Royal engineers and had begun his work as assistant superintendent, limited his vocabulary to only one word to describe the Lotha Nagas: sullen. Although in later years the British administrator–anthropologist J.H. Hutton refuted the tag and said that the 'Lothas were anything but sulky',[64] Woodthorpe was continuing the observations of the previous agents of the empire who were not always friendly towards them.

'Nagas always seem to think that tactics which are successful among themselves will prove equally so against us; they were therefore probably not a little surprised that at the first alarm we did not lose our heads and rush blindly into the jungles, where, of course, they would have got the better of us,' observed Woodthorpe the night they were attacked by the Nagas. Being the first after Captain Brodie to visit this part of the Naga Hills in 1844, he reported of the superiority of their firearms despite the small number of soldiers and only the Khasi, Jaintia and Kuki coolies accompanying them, and about how they defeated and subdued the Lotha Naga villages with '18 dead bodies counted about the village' and their loss 'of course was nil'.[65] For an expanding empire, they had officers gloating over their success in small monographs and reports as well.

The use of guns by the British Army attracted an unprecedented interest amongst the Nagas. There are tales of how intriguing this new weapon was which killed with a fireball from a distance. It was not as if while the British counted the dead bodies of the Naga warriors and exacted submissions from the village chiefs, the Nagas were not dreaming of procuring and possessing the gun and learning to use it for themselves. The British themselves reported in their criminal records as to the number of guns that were either stolen by the Nagas or bought through other subjects of the British government. From John Butler's 'Rough notes on the Angami Nagas',[66] the title itself indicates a tone of fear and respect for the Naga warrior. Titled 'National Offensive Weapons', we would now think Butler was talking about chemical weapons in the Naga Hills but rather he was referring to the spear and the dao used by the Nagas. In note after note and report after report, we have seen how the British feared the spear more than the dao, as it was more likely to inflict a mortal wound than the dao. In fact, Butler himself was ironically killed in 1875 at Pangti by the Lotha Nagas using a spear in a battle between guns and the ancient weapons of the Nagas. The Nagas valued and guarded the spear and the dao with their lives, and John Butler in the same pages wrote in detail about both these 'offensive weapons'; it is clear that the spear and the dao are as much part of the Naga identity as any other aspect of their life. It was therefore no surprise for the British to write about the newfound love of the Nagas for a superior weapon. The desire to acquire firearms reached new heights due to the constant war waged against the aggressors and the inherent need to defend a village. How this contributed to the creation of a political headquarter is also part of the story behind the creation of Kohima and Nagaland.

Already by the 1870s the Angami Nagas were in possession of a considerable quantity of arms, and according to Butler 'an Angami will give almost anything he has for a gun.'[67] With the frequent conflict against the British, it was definitely necessary for the Nagas to fight them with the weaponry used to subdue the Angami Nagas. It was only natural for them to want the firearms and acquire them by any means. There was no justification needed to do that; however, such activities were painted negatively by the British army in their reports. They could not stop the natives from their own desire to protect themselves and attack an enemy.

8

The Bloody Years

From the first expedition to the formation of the Naga Hills district and later to the decision of making Kohima the political and administrative headquarter, it was a gory tale of several battles stretching over several years. The actors from the British East India Company were mostly soldiers ordered to ensure that the policy of non-interference be complied with. It must be noted that the decision to establish Kohima as the headquarters of the Naga Hills district was not an easy one. A decision, if taken earlier, would have saved many warriors' lives. It was also a brutal one. The assertion by superior arms against a brave and courageous tribe would subdue and disperse a community temporarily. However, history has shown that military victory was not sustainable. We will trace the years between 1839 and 1878 wherein the entire gamut of policy shift towards the Naga Hills took shape.

Between 1835 and 1839, the British EIC had just one policy towards controlling the 'hostile Nagas'. They assumed that since the chief Cachari Senapati Tularam and the Manipur kingdom had some degree of 'jurisdiction' over some portions of the Naga areas, they would be engaged to jointly give protection to areas frequently raided by the Tenyimias, especially in the hill villages of North Cachar. They were tasked with establishing a line of posts to protect the British EIC subjects along the neighbouring Naga frontier. Both the Manipur king and Tularam Raja knew from experience that once their forces retreated, the Nagas would come down with such forces as to unleash their wrath over the unprotected subjects and hence the only option was for them to urge the officers of the EIC to establish a permanent post. But due to Gambhir Singh's brutality, the British were also hesitant to allow the Manipur Levy to have a free hand. Every winter they would continue their expeditions to the Naga Hills to plunder and loot the Naga villages. Their winter raids provoked fierce retaliation from the powerful Naga villages. This became an additional headache for the British government. The political agent of Manipur in 1837, Captain George Gordon, was the first to propose another solution to the entire issue. He proposed that the Manipur Levy and the British troops be placed under a 'European' officer. He also proposed in a letter to the Governor General of India that 'its inhabitants are highly capable of deriving benefit from the well qualified Missionaries who might be sent to instruct them in the useful arts as well as in letters and religion, while they, the members of each community being left to govern themselves under the general but immediate superintendence of a European Officer, gradually they would become more and more a happy and united people.' He was seized of the matter as he did not want to take the military approach alone. As we can see, he was the first to come up with the idea to allow the American missionaries into the Naga Hills. Proselytization as a tool to assist colonial domination was mooted.

Captain Jenkins, who had by then become the commissioner of Assam, and given his experience with the Naga hills, offered the British government a new policy. He proposed that the state should pursue 'aggression against the Nagas'.

The Governor–General of India, for reasons of manpower deployment in other areas, did not want to assume direct responsibility for the Nagas. It was only in 1839 that the government at Fort Williams decided to send troops from Assam for an expedition to control and end the raids by the Nagas. It dawned upon the government that neither the Manipur Levy nor Senapati Tularam could be trusted to find a permanent end to the raids.[68]

In 1839 E.R. Grange was chosen, as Lt Lyons could not be spared due to a threat from the court of Ava, to lead the first expedition since the British reviewed their policy towards the Nagas. He was the sub-assistant commissioner stationed at Nowgoan, and was selected to lead a force of around fifty Shan militia and sixty-odd sebundies.[69] Although the first expedition did not amount to any substantial outcome owing to poor supplies and communication, they did make some inroads into the region. Grange managed to gather essential information of the trade routes taken by the Nagas into Assam besides gaining more insights into the structure and polity of the Nagas. The mist of the unfamiliar was thereby dissipated. He was almost on a reconnaissance mission towards the region in his first expedition. The first political headquarters of the Naga Hills was surveyed by Grange. Samaguting, as the British officers called it—a little above the present-day Chumukedima[70]—was placed right at the intersection of the Naga Hills and the Cachar plains. Right on the foothills of Dimapur, it was a strategic location for setting up a station for the British EIC. It was initially a trading centre for salt. If ever there was to be a change in policy to be affected, the location was suitably chosen. The first expedition by Grange exposed the lack of thorough preparation. Not only was the supply insufficient, but the porters were also harassed by a mixture of malaria, hailstorms and unruly weather. Going into unfamiliar territory without proper preparation was not what Jenkins would have wanted. The Governor–General's agent would have desired meticulous planning on the part of Grange. He had the first-hand experience of the first expedition from Imphal to Dimapur in 1831 and had learnt valuable lessons.

Suffice to say that the expedition to investigate the raids was also meant to find ways to punish the two powerful villages of Khonoma and Mezoma. Grange met with the powerful clan chief of Mezoma, who went by the name 'Ikkaree', at his temporary camp. The colourful description of the chief by Grange makes things clearer about him, 'Ikkari, also, the powerful Chief of

Mezoma, who had led most of the raiding parties in Cachar, a perfect savage, wild and suspicious, wearing a collar fringed with hair of his enemies' scalps, came down to see for himself what the camp was like.'

Much of the reports by the British officers were centred on their estimation of the new and unverified territory. What is summarily put as 'raids' was much more than what they meant. The villages of Khonoma and Mezoma were constantly raiding all the neighbouring villages down till North Cachar while at the same time maintaining control over the trade of shells, salt, ivory, horns, beads and tea seeds. These items would come in handy later on in the war with the British as they traded them with the 'avaricious' Kukis of western Manipur for muzzle loaders and 1853 Enfield Pattern rifles.[71]

From the reports on the first and second expeditions of Grange, the attack on the Tenyimia villages resulted in further provocations. What they did not understand was the seriousness with which the villages considered the intrusions. The preparations took months and every able-bodied man was enlisted for the war. For any major confrontation, the villages ensured that the women and children and the frail and the weak were first evacuated to the top of the mountains or to a safe location. With stealth and the swiftness of the wind, the natives had the advantage of knowing the terrain better than the intruders. The British were on an expedition while the natives were fighting to defend their land against unwanted intrusions. It was with the sole intent of defending their way of life. Even the raids on the Naga villages towards North Cachar was considered their historical practice. They even ventured down till Sylhet to trade in salt and slaves. They would capture the vanquished as they raided other villages and sell them as slaves to any buyers in Bengal or the Assam plains. As they say, 'to the highest bidder sold'.

Unbeknownst to the Nagas, the fate of Bengal had changed with the Battle of Plassey. Bengal literally came under the control of the East India Company. The expansion towards the vast hill tracts from Chittagong to the districts of Arakan and Sylhet brought the raids and headhunting to the notice of the British empire. Upon investigation, the British officials found that the raids included plunder, kidnapping and headhunting— and when they could not procure goods they wanted to barter, sometimes the show of might to the plainsmen and neighbours on the hills as well. Kidnapping was to procure slaves. But these raids predate the advent of the Battle of Plassey. Some Europeans started buying lands in Cachar only after they found out that tea plantations could thrive there. The land grab and introduction of workers from across central India to Assam were not in sync with the Naga raids. It interfered greatly with the practice of raids. As the tea plantations went further inside the North Cachar hills, the Nagas increased their raids into the areas occupied by the white tea planters, taking away their labourers as slaves. Slaves captured thus sometimes became part of the community in the Naga Hills. An illustration of the practice of slavery in the nineteenth century is captured by A.W. Davis in his study of the Ao tribe in 1891.[72]

'This custom (slavery) was universal throughout the Ao Tribe. Since our occupation of the country, every effort has been made to suppress the custom, and the selling and buying of slaves is now, I fancy, well treated, being considered almost as members of the family. Cases of harsh treatment, of course, must have occurred occasionally, but these must now be very rare, and the slaves who have remained with their owners know very well that if ill-treated, all they have to do is run away. In Old days slaves, unless they could get down to the plains, could not run away, it being etiquette for them to be caught and returned by the inhabitants of any village in which they took refuge. Troublesome slaves were usually sold to people living across the Dikhu (river) amongst whom the custom of human sacrifices is not, I believe, entirely unknown. Amongst the Aos, before our occupation of the country, slaves were not infrequently paid by one village to another village with which they happened to be on bad terms, to make up a quarrel, and as a sort of set off against any heads taken by them. Slaves paid in this way were invariably slaughtered by the village which recovered them, as an offering to the spirits of the men on their side who had been killed. Female slaves were not allowed to marry or have children. If they became pregnant, their children were killed immediately after birth, or else abortion was procured. Female slaves are not tattooed.'

However, in the Naga practice of slavery, the children of slaves were all considered as slaves.

This description by A.W. Davis of slavery among the Aos elucidates the culture of slavery embedded in their tribe. The elaborate process of how slaves were treated by one village is recorded in his Assam census report on the 'Naga Tribes'. But that was long before the British took over the Naga Hills and the American missionaries began their work.

In fact, the British empire wanted their officers to visit the Angamis from time to time to curb the trading of slaves. In 1841 Lt Bigge made some inroads with the Angami Nagas and had two important agreements. The first was to open a salt depot in Dimapur. The second was to fix the Dhansari River as the boundary between the British districts and the Angami tract. These were major signposts in the history of their engagement.

'The government directed that a repetition of these friendly visits should be made from time to time, mainly with a view to the suppression of the slave traffic carried out by the Nagas with the Bengalis of Sylhet.'

The slave trade was, however, not only limited to those from Sylhet or with the Bengalis. There is an instance of one man from an Angami village selling a girl from another Angami village to the Kukis. The matter was reported by the then chief commissioner, Elliot, on 2 May 1881.

'A Man of Mezomah, who was accused of having sold a girl of Kerumah to the Kookies, was compelled to procure her restoration, and did so.'[73]

In his report on his expedition to the Naga 'territory', E.R. Grange[74] writes that,

'I also applied for a statement of the sufferers of the village of Rangai, but the Raja could not furnish one, as the people had all fled into the jungles, he knew not whither. I was told that the people of Semkar (present-day Semkhor in Dima Hasao, Assam) were also thinking of leaving their village for another, till they heard that troops were going against the Angamis, for they also were in daily fear of being cut up, which they certainly would be the moment they refused to bribe them with salt and dried fish. The Semkar people are not great cultivators, but live chiefly by the produce of their salt springs, and by traffic with the peaceful Nagas around them. They bring dried fish, beads, conch shells, and brass ornaments from Oodarbund Haut, and barter for cotton, wax, ivory, chillies and an extensive and infamous trade is carried on in slaves, who are stolen indiscriminately by all in that quarter, and sold to the Bengali merchants who go up for cotton. I hear that a slave can be procured for twenty packets of salt, seven of which are to be had for one rupee. I saw many Muneeporees, who had been thus seized whilst young, and sold both amongst Kookies, Cacharees and Nagas.'

There was a spiritual aspect of slavery attached to headhunting. Many of the Nagas believed that the skulls of the heads taken during the raids with the objective of adorning the graves of their ancestors would ensure that the spirits of the slain would become the slaves of the ancestors in the spirit world.

'The people killed by a Tongkhul or Luhupa, become his slaves in the next world. Their general religious observation does not differ essentially from those of the Kowpoi tribe.'[75]

During the second expedition, Grange had expected to meet the Manipur Levy who were stationed there in the Naga Hills for more than fifty days, but on arriving at the scene, he found that they had left for Imphal following a shortage of supplies. For the second expedition, he was better armed and supplied. The porters were also better paid and looked after. The 'Jorehath Militia' had already arrived and were placed in charge of the stockade containing the grain. However, the trouble was with the Naga villages. The earlier meeting with the Mezoma village chief did not actually end in a conciliatory agreement despite the ceremony conducted to establish a relation. They were harassed on their way back to Dimapur by the warriors of Mezoma. Despite the lack of casualty on both sides, the provocations remained etched in their minds. The villages were better prepared too but lacked superior arms. They only had intimate knowledge of the terrain, a strongly motivated group of warriors, and the advantage of stealth attacks. They were successful in close combat but were no match for the artillery, mortars and mountain guns of the British.

Another interesting description of the Naga prisoners captured by Grange displays his utter distaste for the Nagas. From Samuguting, he wrote a report to Lt H. Bigge[76] on the harassment met by his force and the tactics used by the Nagas on his troops.

> I have the honor to acquaint you of my having arrived at this village on 23rd instant and that I found the villagers, not-withstanding their pacific professions at Dhemapore, doubtfully disposed towards us. Marks of a barricade having been erected were visible which was no doubt to obstruct our passage, via this route, but on our approach, it had been removed. They had cleared a path through the forest as promised, not in the direction I had ordered them, but took it into the stony bed of the Desem river which added to the annoyance of such a painful route, would have taken us a considerable distance from the village, and placed us in such a position as would have allowed of their annoying us without difficulty . . . On my arrival at the summit of the hill, I found them all assembled with spears in hand but on my threatening them, they put them away, and promised to build us any sheds we required, and assist us in erecting the stockade for the military post, to be established here, after my pointing out the hill I thought best adapted for one, and putting their promise to the test, they refused to do anything and commenced attempting to bully by observing a sulky mood, and saying their spears were their Rajahs and they would assist us in no way.

He nevertheless expressed his joy that none of the detachments that accompanied him were wounded in the attacks, although several sepoys were struck by the spears. They also had a narrow escape from being poisoned. The troops were able to discover a poisonous root submerged in the well before it could properly dissolve. The entire expedition had him on his guard and the letter shows how he fended for his safety.

'I propose taking the prisoners to Nowgong with a view of deterring the other villages from repeating such conduct and should beg to suggest that after a short imprisonment, they should be allowed to return, when they shall have satisfied themselves of the total impossibility of resistance as their *obstreperous* conduct proceeds chiefly from their excessive *ignorance* and *uncivilized* state of existence.' No race would have appreciated such an outrageous description of their ancestors but many reports of the British officers carrying out the violent expeditions in the name of checking and containing the raids and imposing their rule over the Nagas caricatured them in such inglorious terms consistently.

The scale of preparations may have varied but for the next ten years there were yearly expeditions led by various British officers with the sole intent of containing the Tenyimias and having a foothold over this region. The continuous oscillation between conciliation or confrontation, as it would otherwise mean when they interfered directly, contributed towards this protracted period of establishing Kohima as the final headquarter.

In 1841, the proposal for constructing a road across the hills to Manipur was rejected on the score of expense.[77] Lt Bigge, principal assistant in charge of Nowgaon, approached the villages of Punglwa, Mezoma and Khonoma for cessation of hostilities. The Nagas had not forgotten the killing and the burning of their villages by Grange in his second expedition. They nevertheless entered into an agreement with Lt Bigge as to the borders defined by Bigge. The British were concerned about establishing a permanent border demarcation between the Manipuri kingdom and the Nagas and finally a declaration of the extent of British controlled areas.

Some Naga areas were to be brought under British protection. But they did not convey this in a manner that the Nagas would understand. Despite the pledges and the promise of justice by the British, the conciliatory approach was bound to fail from the very start. The road proposal would have been a better strategy despite the expense it would incur as it would have established a permanent presence of the British forces as per the desire of the British EIC. The raids continued as soon as the British left. The salt depot at Samaguting was the only permanent establishment. It highlighted the importance of trade in cultivating a relationship with the Nagas.

The border demarcation imposed on the Manipur king and the Nagas would have repercussions on future relations. Although many factors contributed to the stretching of the attempts to contain the Naga Hills, the British were not particularly poised to see beyond their immediate interest.[78]

For instance, the disgruntlement over the boundary demarcations led some sections of the Manipur Levy to join forces with Khonoma in raiding the villages under British protection. The collaboration between the Naga warriors and the troops of the Manipur Levy raised eyebrows in British political circles. The collaboration sufficiently upgraded the weaponry of the Naga warriors. By the time the alliance was formed, it was possible for the Khonoma warriors to attack the anti-Khonoma khels of Mezoma and subdue them. Long after Lt Vincent in 1849, leading a strong force of the Assam Light Infantry with three pieces of artillery, had secured a position at Mezoma, the attack on the anti-Khonoma khels was considered an affront on the British. In 1844, the British under Captain Eld had attacked and burned down Khonoma village. It is recorded that 500 houses were burned. Captain Eld was the first to find out that the Manipuri troops were assisting the Khonoma village warriors. He would continue the journey of conciliatory expeditions to the Naga Hills begun by Grange. The Manipuri raids did not only target the Naga and Kachari villages in North Cachar but also included attacks on the British outposts. This further enraged the British officers.

The plan under the so-called 'conciliatory expeditions' had several contradictory and unpleasant ramifications. All attacks on the Naga villages were apparently in retaliation to the attacks by the Nagas. It was punitive in nature. And every report used the word 'punitive' rather repetitively. For the Nagas, the constant interference to their raids at the foothill was becoming a nuisance and the various conciliatory visits by the Company officers were proving to be too costly for them. Many young warriors were dying and they were forced to rebuild their villages every year due to the attacks. But these resilient and courageous people were getting accustomed to the new way of life. The rigorous training for the youths was established inadvertently, as the new modes of warfare meant they had to be better prepared. Dispersing and regrouping thus became normal. They would suffer this routine for the next ten years without any respite. In the meantime, the womenfolk had to shoulder the burden of cultivating and bringing in food. But if tradition is anything to go by, it was not something the Nagas were not used to. It was in the culture to adapt to changing circumstances, even if the change was always harsh.

The list of officers who led the expeditions during the period of the non-interference policy is long. Forgotten by the present generations, these officers who traversed the entire continent to serve the empire were also responsible for burning village after village to secure a permanent rule over the Naga Hills. The linguistic variety and the diverse system of village administration perplexed the British officers. On the other hand, the process of conciliation was difficult for the Nagas to comprehend. The policy of 'take no prisoners' during a headhunting expedition was surprising to the British as the raids were markedly different. During these raids the objective was clear: to capture essential commodities was the priority; heads were tradition at best.

There was confusion with the policy of the Governor–General in Council as a result of the attack by Khonoma and the subsequent burning down of the village by Captain Eld. It was punitive and not conciliatory at all as acknowledged by the Council. With the entrance of Major John Butler in 1845 from Sadiya in Assam to the post at Nowgong, a new policy was adopted.[79] With a mix of restraint and conciliation, a partial shift in the approach towards aggressive Naga villages emerged as the new policy. Although not on paper, it was a natural response to the raids. The conciliatory approach would be the first overture, and if attacks were mounted on the British, retaliation would follow. It was under this confidence that Major John Butler first visited the Naga Hills and met with the village chiefs, succeeding to the extent of securing tributes from them. He mapped the topography of the hills in the process.

'Agreements further with the other village chiefs were made that they paid tributes, tendered oaths of allegiances and stopped fighting amongst themselves'. This was the summing up of three years of Butler's visits from 1845–47.[80] The Nagas regarded the oaths with disdain. No concept of oath of allegiance prevailed for long. The affront was seen as temporary. The stealth attacks would continue and all allegiances and oaths were violated with frequent raids and feuds.

9

Pangti, Wokha: Where a Butler Was Speared

In 2021 a young lady from Khonoma village visited the famed Doyang River around Pangti Village for the first time. Due to the Doyang Hydro Electric Project, the reservoir has provided an opportunity for enthusiasts of all kinds—from anglers to boating buffs to adventure lovers—to flock to the tourist location every year for a piece of the gentle river breeze and the delicious river fish cooked with bamboo shoot. The site of the Amur falcons, migratory birds that traverse all the way from Siberia to nest at Pangti Village for their winter sojourn from the end of October to the first week of November, also attracts bird-lovers and conservationists alike. Tents had popped up in several locations to cater to this new breed of tourists. Ornithologists and birdwatchers come from all over India to catch a glimpse of the Amur Falcons soaring around the reservoir. For this they have to get up as early as 4 a.m. It is also the time of the year when the primary inhabitants of Wokha district celebrate their most important harvest festival, the Tokhu Emong.

The young lady was from the same khel and clan as the great warrior defender of Khonoma, Judelie Hiekha. The trip was made to visit the famous tourist spots and outdoor camps at Doyang. Judelie was one of the famous warriors who is said to have been involved in the ambush and killing of G.H. Damant, the first political agent of the Naga Hills district when the headquarters shifted to Kohima from Wokha. According to a handout given to visitors at Khonoma, there is a brief story of his role in the revolt against the British during 1879–80. Here in its twenty-first-century memory, it is mentioned clearly as to who killed Damant, unlike in 1879 when the Khonoma village had resolved not to reveal the name of the warrior that killed Damant. The warriors severed his head and displayed it on a retaining wall in the village. There is however a contestation in the village about the name of the one who shot Damant. Judelie had gone in self-exile after the death of Damant, and the village resolution had led to the secrecy of the village being strictly maintained. Another clan had gone to court as recently as 2020 with regard to the same. Suffice it to say that the great warriors of Khonoma shot and killed G.H. Damant. The story has been told and retold several times over and the legend survives for both the Nagas and the British alike. The narrative from the Semoma khel is that the great warrior Vizerü Rürhie, a sharp marksman, was the one who shot and killed Damant. Ultimately, the entire village came together to guard the forts and attacked the British. Damant would not be the first political officer or deputy commissioner killed on duty. Carnegy, the political officer before Damant, was accidentally shot dead by one of his sentries.[81] Unlike Carnegy, however, both John Butler and Damant were killed by the Nagas. Whereas John Butler was speared at Pangti during a survey and died due to the injury, Damant was shot as he was leading an expedition to Khonoma.

At the riverbank where the green Quechua camping tents were pitched in the shade of the rubber plantations, she met the young entrepreneur who owned the resort where birdwatchers and local tourists alike thronged for the outdoor camping experience. Over several cups of tea, they found out that they had one history in common. They were descendants of warriors who had killed, or had been involved in the attack on, the two famous British officers—the deputy commissioner and the political agent. The moment was captured in a photo produced here in the book.

Captain John Butler was the first to be killed on one such survey expedition at Pangti. Today, the place has been transformed by the construction and commissioning of the Doyang Hydro Electric Project run by the North Eastern Electric Power Corporation Limited (NEEPCO). But to this day, the Pangti villagers will point out the exact spot where Butler was speared. Christianity had not reached the Lotha area as yet and the Pangti villagers had no qualms about defending their land against British intrusions. They were, after all, the largest Lotha village and the warriors decided to ambush the survey party led by Capt. Butler, Lt Woodthorpe and Col Tulloch. The headman of Sanis village had forewarned them about a possible ambush at Pangti but the survey party did not pay much heed. The signs along the path were ominous for the survey party.

It was on a fateful Christmas day that the ambush took place. The spear went right through Capt. Butler's chest to his lungs and he was mortally wounded. The account by Woodthorpe is vivid and in remarkable detail he mentions the harrowing days till the morning of 7 January when Butler finally succumbed to his injuries at Pangti. First aid was given by a native doctor before the arrival of the European doctor from Golaghat. Today, the trip to Golaghat from Pangti takes only about two hours by car. However, it took them a few days to reach Golaghat from Pangti. At the site where he was speared now stands a resting shed in commemoration of Captain John Butler. The place is referred to as Ritssophen Lanrhyu by the locals which roughly translates as 'thoroughfare of the battle' from the Lotha language. It remains a popular conspiracy theory till date that the native doctor was asked to apply a lemon and salt paste over the wounds thus ensuring that the wounds festered sooner than normal. This very act is attributed to be the main cause for his deteriorating condition. He was just thirty-three years old at the time of his death and his grave is still there at the Christian cemetery for the British at Golaghat, Assam.

Butler's death had three significant impacts on the locals and the fate of the Naga Hills district.

If you happen to visit Golaghat today, you will find traces of the event in the bustling city. It is the headquarter of one of the largest districts in Assam and is usually seen as a twin city to Jorhat which is just 55 kilometres away, the last capital of the Ahom kingdom. The Dhansiri River from Dimapur passes through Golaghat to the Brahmaputra. The earliest urban tea centre in Assam, Golaghat also has several heritage buildings. But what is of concern in this chapter is the presence of Assam's first departmental store—Doss & Co.—constructed in 1930 and incorporated under the Registrar of Companies, Shillong.

It is around this departmental store that you will see a slew of ponds. After Butler was wounded at Pangti, the village was burned down three times by the vengeful British forces. All the granaries at Pangti were looted by the British, and the British administration decided to impose a unique punishment on the warriors of Pangti village. They were taken to Golaghat and made to dig the ponds around the present location of Doss & Co.

The second impact of the death of Butler was the shifting of the headquarters of the Naga Hills district to Wokha from Samaguting. Having realized that the location was not healthy for a permanent headquarter, the British decided to shift it. Besides being a strategic location from where they could extend control over the eastern Nagas, Wokha was easier to reach from Golaghat. They could also carry out their expeditions from Samaguting, which would remain an outpost.

Lt Woodthorpe said,[82] 'Wokha is by far the best site, all things considered that could be chosen, and its position renders it exceedingly eligible for a Headquarter station, where the Angamis on the one hand and the eastern Nagas on the other can be easily reached.'

The British were contemplating a first boundary between the Naga Hills and Burma at the same time. It is also ironic that the site decided for Wokha was chosen by Butler during his surveys. He had called the spear and the dao the national offensive weapons of the Nagas. And he was killed by the spear—the national offensive weapon of the Nagas. The great Lotha warrior was Mhonyimo Ngullie of Pangti village.

In the gentle November weather, Robin Ngullie, the great-grandson of the warrior who had speared Butler, met with the descendant of the great warrior Judelie at his resort, The Falcon Creek. They did not know each other's history when they first met. It was a chance meeting which led to further promises of engaging each other in the retelling of the stories of the rebellion against the British forces. The road to building Kohima was a violent one involving their great ancestors.

Of all the stalwarts of the anti-British resistance, the names of the warriors who struck the British officers dead remain etched in the history of the villages from where such heroes emerged. The gradual expansion to all the Naga Hills through the various surveys and expeditions was now accompanied by the activities of the Christian missionaries. While the headquarters were moving upwards to the hills from Wokha to Kohima, the administration was happy that the missionaries were not only making inroads through Mokokchung, they were also aiding the expansion of the British empire into the Naga Hills through the entry of Reverend Clark.

The death of an officer of the British empire was not the sole reason for shifting the headquarter of the Naga Hills district. But it was nevertheless a major event which made the British nervous about their rules of engagement with the Nagas. An excerpt from the Foreign Political Proceedings in 1880 reads thus:

> The new station had been established on a spur connected with the ridge on which the village of Kohima stands, at a distance of about a mile from the walls of the village, on its southern side.
>
> The whole of the buildings of the station, including also the lines of the military garrison and of the police, were enclosed in two irregular shaped stockades close together but not connected with each other, one of which, the western one, contained the

buildings occupied by the civil residents, and by the police, the other being devoted principally to accommodations of the troops, it also contained the Cutchery buildings. The stockades were originally erected by the party of the 44th Regiment under Lieutenant Mc Gregory which accompanied Mr Damant in effecting the occupation, but they are reported to have been in a weak state and the entrance, were still unprovided with doors.

The water supply was provided by an aqueduct constructed by the Kohima Nagas, brought from a distance of nearly two miles from the hills on the south of the station.

Since the occupation of Kohima, the behaviour, of the surrounding Angami Villages had been generally satisfactory, with the exception of Khonoma, the largest and most powerful of all these communities, which maintained an attitude of sulky hostility, at another of treacherous acquiescence.[83]

In November 1878, the headquarters of the Naga Hills district shifted for the third time from Wokha to Kohima. The description of the entire station of the deputy commissioner is clearly suited for an occupying force. The district headquarters is nothing short of a military garrison. Kohima was chosen as the best site for the headquarters since it commanded the principal Angami villages and also the route to Manipur. The entire narrative of the British officers who advocated the shift to Kohima is misleading. Col Keatinge, the first chief commissioner of Assam, is perhaps to be credited as the mastermind behind the move. G.H. Damant was, at best, the implementing officer. The partnership ensured the extension of British rule over the Naga Hills. The consensus opinion among the British officers who sent reports was that the occupation of Kohima was without any opposition. The lack of immediate response to the occupation was no doubt the reason for the assumption. The submission by various villages to the British authority also emboldened the British to assume thus. Kohima assumed the seat of power and authority for the British empire in the Naga Hills. The headhunters could not be tamed without occupation and it was only natural that things would not remain peaceful when the British colonial occupation entered right into the heart of the Naga Hills.

From 1832 to 1878 the interaction had been a long bloody affair and there was no respite from it as the larger Naga villages would not accept the British incursions. Advocating a forward policy, the unwelcomed entry into the heart of the Angami area by the British was resented deeply by the natives. Compared to the nearly five decades of fierce battles, what was going to come in the aftermath of the shifting of the headquarters was larger in scale and far more violent in nature. It was to shape the future of the region in a way neither the British nor the Nagas would have imagined.

The raids continued and the harassment irked the British no end despite the shift to Wokha from Samaguting. The move to Kohima was more a military decision than a political one. Or rather the political was always based on the security and military aspect of the expansion. From the very start it seemed as if Kohima was destined to be the site of unceasing battles where the fate of an empire would be shaped through the sacrifice of many lives. Kohima was wrought in the furnace of violence, as it were.

A tiger was killed by a brave hunter from Khonoma in October 1879. In the celebration of such a feat it was noticed that the guns were aplenty, and decided that the affront of setting up a headquarter right in their alley was not to be taken lightly. Even Samaguting was torturous to the bravehearts. They had been as far as Sylhet to take heads and capture slaves. An impediment of some sorts, they were biding their time and displaying their annoyance at the moves of the British. The Naga warriors did not know of the British policies towards them nor did they care for what the British were discussing in Calcutta or London. All that mattered was the irritant presence of the British and the Manipur Levy which had sufficiently affected their right of conquest.

The spear was used to kill the tiger, but with a stratagem which skilled hunters were known to use to kill something as difficult to hunt as a tiger. Whether it is an elephant or a tiger, the hunters in the village use all the resources available and spend days in the forest before finally launching an attack. Once the animal is sighted, there is an elaborate attempt to encircle the animal and lay a trap by digging a large hole, with the entire village moving in unison with drums and war cries to push the animal to the trap. Celebrations normally led to reflections on their hunting prowess. Any big kill normally became part of a village's folklore.

But unlike the tiger, the provocation came from the deputy commissioner, a scholar and a soldier who wanted nothing less than to dominate all the large Angami villages.

The Dobashi from Khonoma had warned Damant of the impending trouble. Comparisons would be made with his predecessor, Butler, who also didn't heed the warnings of others. Damant was perhaps more casual than usual about fulfilling his Crown duties. He ignored the warning entirely. He was the hunter. Khonoma would be the bounty. The scene for the greatest battle ever mounted against the British empire by the Nagas was set.

10

Scarcity of Salt in the Hills

If there ever was a British officer worth the wit of his Majesty's empire, it would be Francis Jenkins, the then agent to the Governor–General. In the summer of 1846, several hundred warriors from the villages of Kohima, Khonoma, and Mezoma raided the villages from Chumukedima onwards to North Cachar. Hundreds were killed during the plunder and hundreds others were taken captive in the process. The frequency of the raids increased even as the feuds intensified among the Naga villages. Jenkins attributed the entire cause of the raids, feuds and plunder to the 'scarcity of salt in the hills'. Of all the feuds, the one between Khonoma and Mezoma appeared to be the fiercest, engulfing the entire Angami community. It would be reasonable to believe that the British had seen this particular feud as an opportunity to enter into the hills, not only as a protector but also as a mediator. Major Butler's lacklustre involvement during 1845–47 would also be the reason for the outcome of such a process. Conciliation with definite retaliation against any raids perhaps worked in making the British relevant to the smaller villages and enabled them to have a toehold in the politics of this volatile region. Mediation opened the doors for interventions without attracting the grudges of the villages.

Another factor which worked for the British was the heroic presence of a Nocte Naga in the service of the empire. The British first noticed a man called Bhogchand in 1847. Bhogchand is not a Naga name and would have been his nickname through his mother, who was Assamese. He was originally from Namsang under Tirap, presently in Arunachal Pradesh. Employed as a Dobashi[84] or a Naga interpreter by Captain Brodie in 1842, he served as an expert on Naga affairs during the expeditions made in the Namsang Area from 1842–46. He was a native and he worked for the British with loyalty. Major Butler's proposal to establish a military post at Samaguting was due to factors beyond their control. In order to arrest the frequent violation of oaths and agreements, it was necessary to establish a police station at Samaguting. The villagers of Samaguting had also submitted various requests for establishing a military post as they faced the brunt of the incessant raids. Samaguting was ideally located on a gentle mount overlooking the wider plains of North Cachar. The Company officials had one condition and that was to place a native officer in charge of the new post with authority to deal with the Naga villages.

Bhogchand had exhibited his courage during one expedition to Mima village in southern Angami where, under fire from a thousand warriors, he led a small police party of seventeen men to safety. He was resourceful and brave and his loyalty to the empire was unquestionable. He was therefore appointed as the first chief native officer of the British EIC from the Naga community. Till his death at the hands of Nitholey, a clan chief from Mezoma village, he fulfiled the role of a courageous policemen, tracking down violators of peace in the Naga villages with his Shan sepoys, arresting the culprits, and carrying out his duty with diligence and impartiality. He was even successful as a mediator. But he failed to understand the internecine feuds among the different Angami villages. Policing was not enough to deter the feuds, and it would be seen in later years that the confusion over the frequent changes in the policy towards the Naga villages would perplex the British officers in the field and had little impact on the Naga villages' position on the raids. At the same time as the police station was created, the feuds between the villages, especially between Khonoma village and Mezoma village, was changing into something the British had feared and anticipated, but one which they did not imagine would materialize this early. A coalition of sorts was being formed. The obvious reason being the unacceptable intrusions into the affairs of the Naga way of life. The intrusions were indirectly uniting the feuding villages. These feuds were not strong enough to stop such a coalition of anti-British forces from shaping up.

Today, Piphema is a small stop where all traffic from Kohima and Dimapur stops to have tea or the famous Naga dishes. No one would have imagined that the warrior Nitholey had speared the brave Chief Native Officer Bhogchand in the neck at Piphema, thereby killing him during a daring ambush in the night. He would not be the first British officer (native or European) to be killed by the Naga warriors, but his death triggered an immediate response from the Company. As mentioned earlier, the small skirmishes at Khonoma and Mezoma were turning into a larger political game. The support of some parties from Manipur to the large Naga villages in the form of firearms and mercenaries was seen as an anti-British move which could transform the entire region into a hotbed of rebellion. Lord Dalhousie made a final call by rebuking Jenkins for failing to contain the situation before sending a larger military force for a retaliatory expedition against Khonoma and the supporting neighbours. They already had a military stockade at Mezoma with a small detachment. However, it was not able to control the attack and harassment from the Angami villages.

The Anglo–Naga war in the chilly winters of 1850–51 was unevenly fought between a brave and courageous coalition and the superior forces of the 2nd Assam Light Infantry. Whatever resistance was provided by the clan and village coalitions of the Angamis, it was destroyed in the violent war. The Angamis were pounded by superior weapons, and the British officers were able to secure a forced surrender in the form of an agreement from all the Angami villages. Records show that the casualties on the Naga side were nearly a thousand. With barbaric ferocity, it is told in the oral narration of the gruesome tale, the British forces with superior arms managed to subdue the Nagas.

But the story had an unexpected impact. Many villages were able to regroup from the loss and re-establish themselves. The regularity of the incursions had compelled the Nagas to rethink their response. One of the main strategies was to build hideouts in the high mountains for the women and children to be evacuated to during the British attacks. The Japfu Mountain provided a safe refuge for the Naga children. Impenetrable and difficult for any force to mount a campaign, its lofty mounts and steep slopes had an abundance of thick forests to hide the villagers. All the warriors remained on duty in the war.

Whereas the British officers in the battlefield believed that the insolent Nagas had been subdued and thoroughly humiliated, the outcome was not favourably viewed from Calcutta by the officials. The conclusion by Lord Dalhousie was that the 'partial control' policy towards the Nagas was a total failure. In a letter from W. Grey to Major F. Jenkins on 21 February 1851, he was asked to 'immediately withdraw the troops from all Angami Naga villages and to abstain from further interference in the internal feuds of the tribes.' By the end of March 1851, all expeditions and posts were abandoned from the Naga Hills. Even the police post at Dimapur was subsequently withdrawn.

The policy of non-interference brought about the same problems. From 1854–65 the British chose to adhere to the policy diligently in Assam. The same was not applicable to Manipur as it was a tributary state and not a direct subject of British rule and policies established by the EIC. While the raids continued unabated towards North Cachar, with the British recording the violence of the numerous raids, there were no written records of the expeditions carried out by the Manipur Levy on the small Naga villages. To secure tributes from the small villages and to establish a relationship with the more powerful villages, the Manipur Levy sent expeditions every winter between 1854 and 1868.

Given his two expeditions, Lt Vincent noted that in every Angami village there were two parties: one attached to the interest of Manipur and the other to the British, but each only working for an alliance to get aid in crushing the opposite faction. Lord Dalhousie was compelled to send a high government official to assess the situation of the British forces on the ground. The violent offensive had touched big villages like Kikruma, Jotsoma, Kohima, Kigwema, Khonoma and Mezoma. For the moment, Sir H.M. Elliot, who went immediately after what the British termed as the 'Kikruma challenge' to assess the field situation, gave a thumbs up to the troops for killing mercilessly in the battlefield and was only critical of the officers for 'seizure of useless and embarrassing territory'. Nothing can be more derogatory than the usage of such words to describe the land they had been attacking for the last ten years in the form of punitive expeditions.

By abandoning the police post at Samaguting, all effective communications with the Nagas got severed. The incessant raids to harass the villages in North Cachar increased manifold. The British had to handle the situation without interfering. In 1853, Tularam's eldest son Nakulram was killed in the Naga Hills forcing the British to annex Tularam's territory to North Cachar. The defensive outposts created by the British along the plains bordering the Naga Hills rendered no effective barrier against the raids. Various British officers found no single measure to control the raids on the frontier.

The government had seen several governor–generals in between the introduction of the policy of non-interference. The rule of the East India Company had also come to an end in 1858. The political turmoil in the subcontinent was also shaping the new policies of the British government over the north-east frontier. The sepoy mutiny of 1857 was damaging enough for them to reassess their policies towards Assam and the frontiers.

But the entire British government was invested in the supposed wastage of their resources towards maintaining a forward policy to check the 'irritants'. The various adjectives used for the Nagas in the official reports and discussions of the British officers of various categories are juicy insults from the modern days' perspective. A quote from a report[85] on the newly formulated policy: 'The two tribes it is now proposed to subject to civilizing influences, the Nagas and the Shendoos . . . They are, the Nagas especially, the most *inveterate* robbers with whom we have come into contact.'

The British were about to enter into official business with the Nagas with such unfiltered opinions which colonialism afforded them. The entire policy would have little or no burden to the British treasury. In the month of October 1866, Samaguting was again chosen as the site for the headquarters of the new district called the Naga Hills district led by the primary architect of the policy Lt J. Gregory. The British government also decided to reorganize the boundaries of the Naga Hills.

The Council had specific instructions for the new district officer:

> Lieutenant Gregory may take up the proposed position at Samaguting, and do his best by tact and good management, supported by a moderate display of physical force to bring that portion of the hill tract adjacent to the plains in order. He will remember that our main object in having any dealings with the hill people is to protect the Lowlands from their incursions. Instead, therefore, of exerting himself to extend our rule into the interior, he will refrain from such a course.

Thus began the journey of the administrative engagement of the British government over the Naga Hills. Along with the expeditions it is also a tale of shifting capitals in the quest for control over what they deemed as useless territory, finally culminating at Kohima.

11

Losses Suffered by the Nagas under Numerous Expeditions Led by Colonial British Forces

Please note that the list of expeditions provided in the table below is based on the laborious compilations provided in Gordon P. Mills's *Tribal Transformation: The Early History of the Naga Hills*, edited by Achilla Imlong Erdican (Prestige Books International, New Delhi, 2013). Gordon P. Mills had compiled the comprehensive list based on various colonial records and archival works.

	Year	Led by	Size of force	Destination or route	Attacks or punishment	Tribes affected
1.	1827	Manipur Levy	Not available	Mogwye (Nagas, west of Imphal)	4 villages 'subjugated'	Tangkhul, Zemi
2.	1828	Jobraj Suninpreema	400 Sepoys Manipur Levy	Monphui, Khongsang-khool	5 villages 'subdued'	Tangkhul, Zemi
3.	1829	Jobraj Suninpreema	600 Sepoys Manipur Levy	Loohoopa, Cheeng-khong-long	3 villages punished	Tangkhul, Zemi
4.	1830	Beenodo Sing Soobadar	300 Sepoys Manipur Levy	Khambee, Meering, Cheeng-khong-long	1 village punished	Tangkhul
5.	1831	Jobraj Suninpreema	2000 Sepoys	Expedition North of Manipur Border	Tungboom attacked	Zemi, Angami
6.	1832	Capt. Jenkins, Lt Pemberton	700 troops, 800 coolies	Yang, Kenemah (Paplongmai), Samaguting, Mohung Dijong	Many Nagas attacked	Angami, Zemi
7.	1832	Lt Gordon	700 troops	Khonoma, Kohima	Many Nagas attacked	Angami, Zemi, Sema

No.	Year	Leader	Troops	Location/Action	Attacks	Tribes
8.	1833	Raja Gambhir Singh	2000 troops	Kohima, Khonoma	NA	NA
9.	1836	Manipur Levy	1000+ troops	Naga Hills	NA	NA
10.	1839	Lt Grange	50 troops	Cheramah, Mozemah	Some Nagas attacked	Angami
11.	1840	Lt Grange	110 troops	Henima, Chekwema, Togwema, Terriama	Ambushed, half of Khonoma burned	Angami
12.	1841	Lt Bigge	17 troops	Dimapur to Manipur border to explore for road	NA	Angami, Lotha
13.	1841–42	Lt Bigge and Capt. Gordon	NA	Bigge meets Gordon at Mulong to establish boundary	NA	Angami
14.	1842	Capt. A. Vetch	60 troops	Moolong, Tangloong, Jaktoong, Banfera	None	Singpo, Tirap
15.	1842	Capt. Brodie	NA	Diku to Bori	Some attacks	Konyak, Nocte
16.	1842–43	Capt. Hannay	NA	Khetree	NA	Wangcho, Tangsa

			71 troops	Diku to Bori	Trying to settle feuds	Ao, Sema, Lotha
17.	1844	Capt. Brodie	71 troops	NA	NA	Rengma, Angami
18.	1844	Mr. B. Wood	NA	NA	NA	Angami
19.	1845	Eld and Wood	50 Shan militia	Khonoma	3 villages burned	Angami
20.	1845–46	Capt. J. Butler	100 troops	Khonoma	None	Angami
21.	1846	Capt. Brodie	NA	Changnon, Tangroong	None	Tangsa, Wangcho
22.	1846–47	Capt. J. Butler	NA	Mozemah	None	Angami
23.	1847	Bhogchand	17 police	Mozemah	Ambushed by Nagas	Angami
24.	1849	Bhogchand	33 police	Mozemah	Bhogchand murdered	Angami
25.	1849–50	Lt Vincent	200 troops	Khonoma	Khonoma burned, Nilholey burns Mozemah Vincent remains over wet season at stockade near Mozemah	Angami
	1850	Lt Vincent	100 troops	Near Mozemah		

No.	Year	Leader	Troops	Location	Result	Tribe
26.	1851	Major H. Foquett and Capt. D. Reid	440 troops 730 troops	Khonoma Mozemah	Khonoma fort destroyed Kenemah (Paplongmai) fined	Angami
27.	1854	Manipur Levy	1500 troops	Kohima, Mozemah	Mozemah destroyed	Angami
28.	1855	Manipur Levy	NA	Mozemah	Mozemah tribute collected	Angami
29.	1866	Lt Gregory	20 police	Samaguting	Razapemah occupied	Angami, Zemi
30.	1868	Lt Gregory	59 police	Razapemah and residents not permitted to return	Razapemah destroyed	Angami, Zemi
31.	1868	Manipur Levy	1000 troops	Kohima tribute collected	Kohima occupied	Angami
32.	1868	NA	NA	Expedition details not known	NA	NA

33.	1872–73	Major Godwin-Austen	150 troops 600 troops	Manipur Naga Hills Boundary survey	Many Naga tribes attacked	Angami, Mao
34.	1873–74	Capt. Badgley	70 troops	Kohima	NA	NA
35.	1874–75	Capt. Butler and Lt Woodthorpe	NA	Survey party to Wokha	Nagas attacked	Lotha
36.	1875	Lt Holcombe and Capt. Badgley	NA	Survey party on Seebsugar frontier	Lt. Holcombe and 80 troops killed at Ninu	Konyak
37.	1875	Col Nuthall	392 troops 70 police 485 collies	Ninu	Ninu burned	Konyak
38.	1875–76	Capt. Butler and Lt Woodthorpe	NA	Survey party beyond Wokha	Capt. Butler killed in ambush at Pangti	Lotha
39.	1876	Lt Woodthorpe	NA	Pangti	Pangti burned	Lotha

40.	1877–78	Capt. W. Brydon	200 troops 50 police	Mozemah Carnegy accidentally shot and killed, terms imposed on Mozemah	Khonoma attacked	Angami
41.	1878	Mr Damant (to Kohima) Mr Hinde (to Wokha)	NA	Posts at Kohima and Wokha occupied	NA	Angami, Lotha
42.	1878	Manipur Levy	NA	NA	NA	NA
43.	1879	Mr Damant	21 troops 65 police	Khonoma	Naga siege of Kohima	Angami
44.	1879–80	Gen. Nation and Col Johnstone	2000 troops	Relief of Kohima destroyed, Jotsoma partially burned	Khonoma attacked	Angami
45.	1882	Mr McCabe	NA	Philimi	Punished for murder of two Lothas	Sema

46.	1883	Mr McCabe and Lt Boileau	75 troops	Ralami	Semas resisted; 50 or 60 Nagas killed	Sema
47.	1887	Mr A. Porteous	40 troops 80 police	Pihupurena, Tirhephima, Sasilimi, Kichilimi	Raiding villages fined	Sema, Angami
48.	1887	Mr A. Proteous	50 police	Nunkum, Are, Man-grung	To hear murder case	Ao, Sema, Lotha

Part II

The Kohima stone erected by Raja
Ghambir Singh, 1833

The mushroom-domed pillars of the Kachari Kingdom in Dimapur

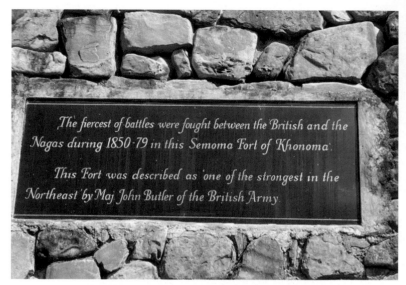

Inscription at the Semoma Fort of Khonoma

Inscription in Khonoma by the Khonoma Thevomia Union in honour of
their warrior Jüdelie Hiekha

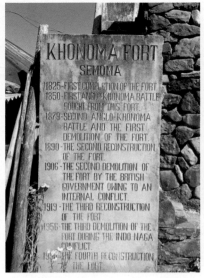

Inscription by the Semoma khel on
the history of Khonoma

Memorial of G.H. Damant
in Khonoma

The shield of the warriors in
Khonoma village

The author holding a 7-foot
muzzle loading gun in Khonoma

Epitaph of an unknown soldier at the Kohima War Cemetery

The only Naga to have a memorial at the Kohima War Cemetery:
Saliezu Angami was a sepoy in the Assam Regiment

The only Mizo to have a memorial at the Kohima War Cemetery: He was a naik at the Assam Regiment

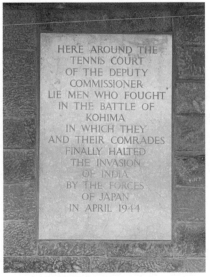

Inscription at the Kohima War Cemetery

The world-famous epitaph at the
Kohima War Cemetery

The house where Lt Gen. Sato stayed in Kigwema village

Inscription on a modern Morung in Kigwema village mentioning the arrival of the Japanese forces

The lodgings of Lt Gen. Sato is now House No. 021, Kigwema village

Viketuno Hiekha with Robin Ngullie:
Descendants of warriors

12

Bone Collectors

'That there's some corner of a foreign field
That is forever England.'

—Rupert Brooke

One fine morning, I got a phone call from someone in the department of the arts and culture, Government of Nagaland. The officer on the other end of the line told me that the Japan Association for Recovery & Repatriation of War Casualties (JARRWC) wanted to visit my official residential quarter to excavate and dig for the mortal remains of dead Japanese soldiers in the garden. These Japanese soldiers died a long time ago, during the Second World War. The visit was in 2019. This was exactly seventy years after the famous Battle of Kohima. There is something about the martyrs or simply the death of their Naga ancestors that haunts an entire generation. Tradition demands that the dead buried far off from home can be brought back long after the interment. The exhumation process is usually carried out to restore the soul to its rightful place, which is naturally the village of origin of the dead individual. According to Naga beliefs, the spirit of the dead is like a seed and the greater the dead's achievement, the more important it becomes to bury the deceased in their birthplace. As recently as 2017 there is an instance of a Naga village in Phek district of Nagaland, called Kutsapo, performing one such rite.[86]

> In a landmark event, the community of Kutsapo village under Phek district finally realized their long-awaited wish by bringing home the mortal remains of Late Sonetso Esan from Darjeeling after forty-eight years since he died.
>
> Esan, a pre-university arts student of St Joseph College, Darjeeling, had died in an unfortunate accident on 18 October 1969 while pursuing his studies and was buried at Bhanu Gram Protestant Cemetery in Darjeeling, informed a press release from Kutsapo Students' Union. The youngest son of Late Kuhuso Vadeo, Esan was the first matriculate from Kutsapo and was also the first designated students' union president of the village.
>
> The grave exhumation project was carried out under the initiative of Kutsapo Students' Union (KSU) led by its president Dr Nutazo Lohe, an assistant professor of Phek Government College.
>
> While keeping the record of Esan's achievements and contributions as visionary leader and a pioneer in the field of education, the grave exhumation project was also carried out coinciding with the forthcoming KSU Golden Jubilee celebration cum seventieth General Session of Chakhesang Students' Union scheduled in January 2018 at Kutsapo village.
>
> Amid utmost due tribute and homage paid by the community as a whole, Esan was finally laid to rest in a grand manner in his own native soil at Kutsapo village on 17 December with all necessary post-exhumation memorial rites, the release added.

The worth and the value of the seed is thereby reborn in the same village by giving it the right burial.

In an uncanny similarity with this Naga tradition, even the Japanese had not forgotten their dead compatriots, and they were persistent in conducting the exhumation process, notwithstanding the loss at the battle of Kohima so many years ago. They came to forage whatever they could find in memory of the soldiers who did not make it back home—the soldiers who died in the battle of Kohima and Imphal in April 1944. The JARRWC termed the search operations as important 'considering the sentiments of the bereaved families of those deceased Japanese soldiers, some of whom have reached a very advanced age, prompt recovery of the mortal remains of the dead soldiers have become top priority of the visiting delegation.'[87] Exactly how they were going to do that was a curiosity for the Nagaland government which had extended all possible support to the mission.

The landscape since 1944 had changed drastically. The Nagas did not retain the memories of the location of the dead Japanese soldiers. No exact direction could be given of the location of the dead. They were killed in the war by enemies' bullets and bombs, and a few died of malaria, dysentery, cholera and starvation. The Japanese war veterans spoke of the search for the remains from the heart: 'Going back to visit our dead comrades, whose graves are covered with moss in the middle of the jungle, is the duty of the survivors, and the fulfilment of the oath we took.'[88] Repatriating the mortal remains was a movement not only among the war veterans but also among the family members of the soldiers. The forgotten war and the damning defeat of the Japanese in the Second World War at the battle of Kohima were post-war issues in Japan that not many in Nagaland were aware of. The search for the grave sites came to nought as it had been ages since the first Japanese soldier died in Kohima. Just when we thought the Japanese efforts to identify and repatriate the remains of the fallen soldiers had ceased, the appearance of this association in Nagaland came as a surprise.

It was in 2019 that the Nagaland government held the commemoration of the seventy-fifth anniversary of the Battle of Kohima under the theme, 'Remembrance, Reconciliation and

Rebirth.' While the word 'Rebirth' was odd in the theme, the ceremony was interesting to watch and the speeches were even more enlightening in their attempt at fostering the nature of the theme. The presence of both the ambassador of Japan to India, HE Kenji Hiramatsu and the high commissioner of UK to India HE Sir Dominic Asquith, KCMG,[89] at the same event was significant on this commemorative event. Descendants of both the Japanese army and the British forces were also present at this event. In a rather emotional reflection of the war, HE Kenji Hiramatsu said, 'We all should never forget that the peace we enjoy today has been built over tremendous sacrifices of the past. Squarely facing the history of the past, Japan renews its commitment never to repeat the devastation of World War II. We look back in order to look towards the future.' He stressed on genuine reconciliation and the need to work tirelessly towards that. Lt Gen. Sato would be smiling from above at this conciliatory speech. The ambassador ended his speech by stating that the relationship between Japan and the north-eastern region had become 'substantially closer'. This aligned with the third part of the theme, 'Rebirth'.

The Japanese had actually observed the anniversary of Kohima in Tokyo on 26 June 1965, wherein 700 survivors of the 58th Regiment gathered at the Yasukuni Shrine for a memorial service. It was the twenty-first year of the battle of Kohima. The members of the Regimental Society formed by the survivors even made considerable efforts to contact, without much success, the British soldiers who fought in the battle. For the Japanese soldiers the nostalgia for Kohima was something beyond hate and love. And this anniversary was being held in Kohima after seventy-five years and with two hitherto unseen occurrences: i) both the British and the Japanese governments were participating, ii) with even some surviving war veterans or their offspring present.

On the other hand, and in keeping with the British narrative, Sir Asquith lauded the courage and sacrifice of the soldiers who had laid down their life. 'Today India, Japan and the UK stand together as three great democracies. We work with each other for peace and prosperity globally, and as committed to facing today's challenge in partnership.' He also paid tribute to the soldiers who sacrificed their lives and the Naga non-combatants who died valiantly supporting the successful defence of the Kohima Ridge against the numerically superior force.'[90]

Among the veterans at the commemorative event was Richard Dey, who had returned to Kohima to see the place where he once fought for his life and the Allied forces. He was part of the Royal Welch Fusiliers assigned to the second division. His reflections on the war he fought and survived can be summed up in his gratitude towards the Nagas. 'Had it not been for them picking up the rifles, I would not have been here.'[91] He was ninety-two years old in 2019 which meant that he was only a teenager when he joined the war in Kohima.

When the Japanese were defeated at Kohima, the commander of the Japanese 31st Division, Lt Gen. Kotuku Sato wrote a farewell message to his troops,

It is clear that this operation was scheduled by the foolish desire of one man: Lt Gen. Mutaguchi, commander of the 15th Army. I do not intend to be censured by anyone. Our 31st division has done its duty. For two months we have defended our positions against a strong enemy force; and not one of their men during that time passed down the Imphal road.

Before God I am not ashamed.

Now I must say good-bye to you. I remember the hard time we had at Kohima and how you helped me do my duty there. I thank you all sincerely.

Our swords are broken, and our arrows gone. Shedding bitter tears, I now leave Kohima. I ask the forgiveness of those who lie dead at Kohima because of my poor talent. Though my body is parted from them, I shall always remain with them in spirit. Nothing can separate those of us who were tried in the fire at Kohima.[92]

Sato was sacked after the defeat at Kohima by Lt Gen. Mutaguchi. After this, he was offered a gun to salvage his honour, but Sato refused to use it. It must have been devastating for a man of immense pride and viciousness. When the Japanese team arrived at my quarters, I recalled the stories we were told by our elders about Sato and his 15,000 strong men camping in Chakabama, Viswema and Kohima to launch the attack on the British forces in Kohima.

Various books written on the battle of Kohima vividly portray the part played by the British forces in defeating the Japanese but also the entire Burma Campaign during the Second World War. In fact, the British National Army Museum voted the Battle of Kohima and Imphal in 2013 as 'Britain's Greatest Battle' over and above the Battle of Waterloo, the Normandy landings and Stalingrad. Ironically enough, the battle of Kohima is often referred to as the 'Stalingrad of the East' in keeping with the trend to situate historical events within a context which the audience in the west can identify with. Almost 90 per cent of the accounts available on the Battle of Kohima are written by the British, American or even non-Naga writers focusing primarily on the experiences of the British and the Allied forces. Even the Japanese have not done much in this regard. There have been attempts by local authors to write about the three months of 'siege' as it were, but most of the authors wrote on the battle of Kohima and Imphal under the empire's shadow.

The Japanese visits to the land where their grandparents died in the thousands under hapless circumstances, just when we thought the war was forgotten, sparked a renewed interest in the forgotten war seventy-five years after it happened. The recognition by the National War Museum of the Battles of Kohima and Imphal raises important flags in the narratives of the internationally significant war. For the world and the British empire, it was a battle with great historical significance, but for the Nagas at the centre of the battle, it was a devastating war they never imagined they would see. This war brought Kohima into the midst of a great global war.

The two events seek to review the greatest battle to have ever happened in different ways. One is to repatriate and the other to commemorate. The difference is itself a clear reference to the varied ways in which the British and the Japanese view the event. A defeat which signalled the end of Japanese control of the Burma–China–India theatre, but one which the Japanese are still struggling to come to terms with due to the sordid nature of the war.

The visit of the ambassador of Japan and the high commissioner of United Kingdom on the seventy-fifth anniversary of the bloody war—where the lives of the Nagas were torn apart like never before and where they were forced to upgrade their heroics from the 1879 'siege' to the global theatre of war they were not accustomed to—was well appreciated as part of the effort to trump up the significance of this war. The beautifully well-maintained war cemeteries by the Commonwealth War Graves Commission and the epitaph itself on the Kohima war cemetery are the only famous remnants today. Indeed, a piece of England forever. One would think that even if the Emperor of Japan did not come for the seventy-fifth anniversary, the Queen of England should have come herself or should have sent her son the prince to the commemorative event in Kohima. It is an indication of where the empire is placed in the new world order. There are many who see the connection between the names given to both the colonial army that fought in Kohima and the war itself as ominous—the 'Forgotten Army' and the 'Forgotten war'. The sobriquets themselves were a commentary on the entire event. While the Japanese have written about their role in the Battle of Kohima and have much less to say about Nagas in that war, the British veterans have been unanimous in their appreciation of the contribution of the Nagas towards their victory in the war.

Field Marshal Viscount William Slim writes in his *Defeat into Victory*,[93] published in 1956, with effusive praise about the Nagas:

'These were the gallant Nagas whose loyalty, even in the most depressing times of the invasion had never faltered.'

The British, to this day, visit this corner of a foreign land which is forever England.

Stories abound in the hearts of the Naga populace of how the war tore apart the land they tilled to live as village republics. The British brought with them a firm hand of administration in the Naga Hills and along with colonialism, they brought war upon the Nagas. This story has been told by some British soldiers and writers, but they are very few and not enough to make this battle heard across the world. And the story will remain buried until we narrate the heroism of a people who did not take sides for the sake of the empire, but for their own survival, as the nineteenth-century invasion of the Naga Hills by the British has shown.

13

General Sato: 'Capture Kohima at Once'

The first thing to do was to build a camp to sleep. As the commander, he had to sleep in a proper hut and not a tent. It represented an air of authority and security. The fifty-one-year-old commander of the 31st Division, Lt Gen. Kotuku Sato, was on a mission to capture Kohima within the shortest possible time. And even as the rations and supplies were arranged for his troops he was critical of the extent to which they would be sufficient. A timeline was envisaged and a very bold decision made to carry only the supplies and provisions required to achieve success within that timeline. To storm into Kohima and capture the small patch of land manned by the British forces was the only agenda. His reputation preceded him. He was instrumental in the defeat of the Russians by the Imperial Japanese Army. There were no doubts about his prowess on the battlefield and the fact that he would be able to accomplish the mission was already assumed as a foregone conclusion. His superior Lt Gen. Mutaguchi was assured of the success. Although they had differences about the mission, the General knew that once Kohima was captured and the British forces stationed in Imphal were attacked from the rear through the road to Imphal from Kohima, the supplies of the enemy forces would be cut. He marched from his temporary headquarters at Homalin, a small town in north-western Myanmar on the River Chindwin, through the vast and impenetrable terrain towards Kohima.

There are lots of academic debates now as to whether he should have just gone down to Dimapur[94] and captured the railway station instead of fighting to dislodge the British from the Kohima ridge after having occupied Kohima village and the Aradura Spur.[95] But fate had different plans for the man. He himself was not satisfied with the turn of events. The ifs and buts did not win him the war. In the end his decision to retreat from Kohima and go back to Japan was a rather unusual thing to do for the Imperial Japanese Army. That decision alone shaped his fate in the history of Japan.[96] He chose to be court-martialled rather than be dismissed from service or commit suicide. Lt Gen. Sato was a man of obstinate character, both on the battlefield and in his dealings with the orders from his superiors. Fate is what saved him as the government at Tokyo saw his court-martial as a sign of disunity in the rank and file of the army, and feared that the general perception would fall low and harm their political situation even more. As a case of madness induced by a post-traumatic stress disorder, he was sent to Java as an attachment to the headquarters of the 16th Army. His quarrel with Mutaguchi is the stuff legends are made of, still unresolved even years after they both died. It is sometimes a topic for discussion among fans of the Battle of Kohima as to how the two Japanese Generals died. Sato, it seems, died of liver cirrhosis in 1958. Mutaguchi died of a stroke nine years later in 1966 at the age of seventy-seven. When the ammunition and the rations were both exhausted by late May, all the commanders sent requests to Mutaguchi for a full withdrawal. But he refused by issuing a directive. 'Continue in the task until all of your ammunition is expended. If your hands are broken, fight with your feet, if your hands and feet are broken, use your teeth. If there is no breath left in your body, fight with your spirit. Lack of weapons is no excuse for defeat.'[97] When Sato died in his hometown Amarume, it is said that the entire family and friends of Sato were shocked to see Gen. Mutaguchi appear at the funeral, distraught and guilt-ridden, muttering apologies to the dead body.

Any sane commander would have well been livid. And a man of Gen. Sato's temper even more so. By the time Sato made the second request for withdrawal, he had already lost 3000 soldiers and had 4000 wounded soldiers in his camp. More than the ammunition, he needed provisions and medical aid. Even the request for air dropping the provisions was turned down by Mutaguchi. He was exasperated. Since leaving Chindwin for Kohima, he noted, they had not received one bullet nor a grain of rice from Mutaguchi.[98] Thereafter when he finally sent a message to Mutaguchi of his withdrawal, it was not a request but a blunt statement. Sato gave a practical reason to Mutaguchi when he finally decided to withdraw from Kohima: 'We have completely used up ammunition for mountain artillery and heavy infantry weapons. The division will therefore withdraw from Kohima by 1st June at the latest and move to a point where it can receive supplies.' Sato radioed in. Mutaguchi, not one to mince words, replied, 'Withdraw and I will court-martial you.'

As expected from a man like Sato, his response was equally feisty. 'Do as you please. I will bring you down with me.' He no longer cared what his superior Mutaguchi might do for his insubordination.

On their watch, more than 50,000 soldiers died or were injured in Imphal and Kohima. And those that could return did so when Gen. Sato finally decided to disobey the orders of Mutaguchi and withdrew his forces from Kohima in late May. Mutaguchi was as harsh a General as he was high-handed. From the very beginning, Sato had the courage to stand up to Mutaguchi and express his scepticism of the plan to capture Imphal and Kohima. Especially when the shortage of supplies was part of the design, the plan was doomed to fail from the beginning. Mutaguchi would later pin the blame on Sato for the loss at Kohima. But historians are clear that the supplies were meant to last only 15–20 days and the dependence on the locals in Kohima and the Naga Hills for support was an irresponsible decision.

Defeat was already wired into the plan. Lack of supplies and the lack of enough artillery was suicidal in the face of better trained soldiers of the 2nd Division, the 161st Indian Brigade and the 33rd Indian Brigade of the British forces.

War entails untold horrors, and the battle of Kohima was no less a bloody affair. However glorified the objectives may have been, the quarrel of these two eccentric army generals of the Imperial Japanese Army would lead to the most disastrous defeat of Japan during that period and in the end their quarrel did not matter. Remembrance is an act not only of the burden of history we each carry in our hearts and minds but also a review of what happened to the thousands of lost souls, as in this case, and it is befitting to appreciate the insanity that humanity walks through for a victory over the other. Nagaland would never be the same again after the Battle of Kohima. Having never seen a plane, the war would bring in not just 'giant flying objects' dumping provisions from the skies to the Allied forces, but also flying birds dangerously dropping bombs on the Japanese camps and soldiers. Unexpected as it was sudden, the glory that both the British and the Japanese forces sought in Kohima was not on the agenda of the Nagas. The colonial deputy commissioner of the Naga Hills was Charles Pawsey, a tall man who was an old hand in the Naga Hills. His administration had anticipated the invasion of the Japanese. This was to be the second siege of Kohima albeit in different circumstances and almost a century apart. The natives had been tamed as it were and they would side with the British this time round.

Only the native son of Khonoma was clear about which side he took. A.Z. Phizo, the future president of the Naga National Council was in Rangoon when Burma fell to the Japanese forces. And Kohima was the next target. It would seem that the British had colonized the Naga Hills and established the headquarters at Kohima only to see it under 'siege' from all quarters. Whereas, in the nineteenth century, the Nagas, especially the Angamis, had formed a conglomeration to retake what was their place and chase away the occupation forces, the Battle of Kohima in 1944 was for a different goal. The first fierce resistance to the British occupation was brutal and led to the death and destruction of many Nagas, ensuring the domination of the British over the Naga Hills. The second was also a challenge to the hold of the British over Kohima, but it was of a very global proportion and could not be compared with the first 'siege'. The Europeans brought the war to the Naga Hills. The Japanese came in pursuit of a much larger dream of domination based on some assumptions about colonial India.[99] The Japanese tried to approach the Nagas with the idea of a common race—'we are all mongoloids they said'. Both Phizo and Subhas Chandra Bose sided with the Japanese for this battle of Kohima. Once Kohima fell it would be an easy march to Delhi. With that the British empire would be thrown out of India. At least that was the dream the Japanese hoped to achieve.

At fifty-one Lt Gen. Sato was an experienced and seasoned hand of the Imperial Japanese Army. By contrast, Mutaguchi, his immediate army commander in the field was older and in comparison not as illustrious as Sato. Later when Sato was dismissed, he didn't take it well. 'This is shameful,' he burst out. 'If Mutaguchi considers himself a knight, he should apologize for his own failure to the dead soldiers and the Japanese people. He should not try and put the blame on his subordinates.' Mutaguchi and his staff maintained that Sato's decision to withdraw was to blame for the disaster that ensued. When the British 2nd Division cleared the last of the Japanese roadblocks and opened the Kohima–Imphal road, the war was lost.

The stark reality facing his division was not lost on Sato. He exhorted his men, 'The enemy are superior in weapons and firepower. Each and every man must look after his rifle as a mother her child. An uncared-for arm is a criminal offence, and any found with an unserviceable rifle, or no rifle at all, will at once be shot by his officer. You will fight to the death. When you are killed, you will fight on with your spirit.'[100]

This was before he ordered the withdrawal. It was futile to exhort his soldiers for any further heroics. It was time to go home.

Gen. Slim was dismissive of Sato as a war commander. 'He is without exception, the most unenterprising of all the Japanese Generals I encountered. His bullet head was filled with only one idea—to take Kohima. He could by 5 April, have struck the railway with the bulk of his division. But he had no vision, so as his troops came up, he flung them into attack after attack on the little town of Kohima.'[101] Gen. Slim, of course, had no inkling of the orders not to move to Dimapur. Sato gambled for the conservation of energy and ammunition for his men. Kohima was the target for him.

There is another interesting anecdote mentioned by Keane in his books that evokes a sense of affection for Sato, despite his tough demeanour. 'An officer of the 138th Infantry Regiment who served with Sato at Kohima wrote an affectionate account of his commander. 'It is evident that My Lord Sato's face is round. His nose is like rice dumpling. His eyes are slightly sharp. Due to such a facial feature, you may imagine that he laughs in such a large-hearted way but the truth is that he giggles with pipe in his mouth. It was one of his uniquenesses to giggle when he made the other person puzzle and face a predicament. When it is funny, he lets his body roll back and laughs "Ha, Ha, Ha" shaking his big belly. My Lord Sato was a funny person.'[102]

As a leader he was not bereft of emotional outbursts when something pricked him. There is this famous story about him: While taking a bath in his bathtub at Kigwema village, a young officer who had come from the war in Kohima was offered a bath in Sato's personal bathtub. The young soldier refused his General's offer with a polite 'thank you' and added that he would not do so as he thought of his men in the battlefield. This touched a raw nerve in Sato and he retorted at his offer. 'You don't know my feeling. As a division leader, of course I would let all men in front line take bath if possible. Realistically, my wish does not come true, so at least I want you to take a bath on behalf of the others.'[103]

It is ironical that while he enjoyed the pleasures of a bathtub in the battle, his post retirement life was not so comfortable. He came back to Amarume, in what is now part of Shonai town, without a home of his own and had to stay at his brother's place in an annexe.[104] There was no bathroom in the annexe and the general had to cross over to his brother's place to use the facilities. It was a far cry from even the small luxuries he enjoyed while in service. Falling on bad times financially and forever haunted by the ghost of Kohima he took refuge in excessive drinking in his last days.

In spite of the sorrow displayed during Gen. Sato's funeral, Gen. Mutaguchi never wavered from his position against the withdrawal by Gen. Sato and continued to blame him for the 'terrible error in leadership'.[105] 'Mutaguchi even cited Slim's criticism of Sato in his list of charges, and then berated Kawabe for holding him back from Dimapur. But the 31st Division veterans were loyal to Sato and forty years after Kohima they finally erected a memorial to Sato in Amarume.

For all the hardships at Kohima and the humiliations thereafter, Lt Gen. Sato never forgot the memory of his division in Kohima. For his part, Satō continued to insist until his death in 1959 that the actions he took were necessary to save the lives of his men, and that the charges of insanity made against him for withdrawing from the battle were unjustified. Sato devoted his efforts to assisting surviving members of his former command, and he created a group of ex-army men who erected a monument to the fallen soldiers of the Kohima/Imphal campaign in Matsuyama, Ehime and in Shonai, Yamagata prefecture.

14

Generals and Commanders

The British came with their troops to station themselves in the various locations favourable to them as per their military policy and strategy. Jotsoma village was one of the main locations correctly identified by the British forces. From there, right at the base of the Puliebadze peak, the British sentinels could see the entire stretch of Kohima. This was in fact the most feasible and advantageous position which could secure the Allied forces a strategic location to launch an offensive upon the enemy lines. For the Nagas, both the American and the British soldiers were the same. They were white and tall and all of them wore military fatigues. They would fire their cannonballs and the villagers could see the Japanese positions being targeted from afar. From a distance, they only saw the smoke spiralling up from the forests. Even a slight scream heard from a distance would invite perceptible applause from the British troops and a sense of awe from Naga onlookers. The forests were being pounded by incessant firing of cannon balls. Death and destruction could be seen from afar.

Kohima was plunged into a horror of explosions which destroyed the entire span of what was then a nondescript small patch of land. The villagers could not go to their fields for cultivation and were restricted from carrying out their normal activities.[106] The war had changed their routine and their lives. Now, they were accustomed to the white soldiers in khaki and the guns blazing in Kohima. The villagers, having no other activities to while away their days, kept themselves busy by helping the white soldiers do their chores and assisted them with whatever they could. Even spying for the British became a lucrative business. Anyone who could bring important information about the movement of the Japanese soldiers was given 300 rupees as a reward.[107] In the initial days of the invasion, there were some Japanese soldiers who nearly infiltrated their village and there is a report of one villager being killed in the event. The death of the villager created a deep sense of fear among the others and they started organizing security in the village. They gathered in the Morung, the traditional tribal dormitory, and the entire village slept together at several hiding places and in the trenches they had dug for the colonial British army.

According to oral narratives collected by Reverend Savito Nagi in his book *Reminiscing the Battle of Kohima 1944*, the British army had issued certain monetary rewards for the Nagas. If a Japanese officer was captured alive, 1000 rupees was to be given to the villager. If the villager captured a Japanese soldier of any other ranks below, the reward was 500 rupees. For a dead Japanese officer, the reward was 100 rupees while a dead Japanese soldier would fetch 50 rupees for the villager. Interestingly enough, a person who was not a Japanese but hostile to the British, if reported or brought, would fetch the villager a handsome amount of 75 rupees. A dead hostile would also bring him a reward of 25 rupees. The entire operation was incentivized by the British and attracted the Nagas to do their best to earn the rewards offered. It was critical since they could not till their fields and were dependent on the food supplies of the British army. The supplies were therefore not only for the British but also for the local population.

The Dimapur railway station was used to bring provisions, food supplies as well as military reinforcements. There were no roads. The railhead at Dimapur was built in 1903 along the Lumding-Dibrugarh section under the then Assam Bengal Railway. Dimapur was critical for the defence of the British empire.[108] From Slim's own words it was clear that although the battles were being fought in the hills of Kohima, holding on to Dimapur was crucial for the success of the Burma campaign.[109] Even the Japanese wanted this position and in fact Mutaguchi proposed the same but was denied by Gen. Kawabe, who stated that Kohima was the only objective for now. This was to prove costly to them.[110] Although Dimapur was the main base for all logistical and supply purpose, the British army was not very fond of the weather. As early as April, it was a base with more coolies than soldiers.[111] All the action took place from Kohima towards Burma.

In and around the Naga hills the villagers were displaced due to the fierce fighting. They fled to safe areas and even found work and were fed well by the British. The Nagas could enjoy the meal as it included dry meat and preserved vegetables in tin containers[112]. To look through binoculars at the Japanese positions was something they had never experienced. In awe of the new tools of war which were nothing like the basic ones they had seen in the past, the Nagas were amazed and uncertain of their fate at the same time.

As the Japanese traversed the entire Saramati Range towards the Japfu range to reach Kohima, war entered the Naga soil in a very unwelcome manner. The refugees were a sign of things to come as discussed in the earlier chapters. Logistical issues were addressed when the Japanese came. The Nagas had witnessed their march and the oral narration of the Nagas is so unlike the accounts from the many reports of the British or even the Japanese. From various sources and through discussions with various individuals in addition to the excellent personal oral accounts collected by Rev Nagi in his book,[113] a Naga chronology of the Japanese invasion and the British defence can be narrated. It is an account of fear and nostalgia, of experiences valued immensely due to their unprecedented violence and the global impact of the war. Nagi, in his book, gave a succinct and comprehensive chronology of the turn of events that led to the Battle of Kohima.

Leaving aside the journey from Homalin in Myanmar, the entry into Nagaland can be easily traced. The Japanese troops occupied Zhavame on 1–2 April 1944 in the present-day Phek district of Nagaland. By 3 April, they had already advanced to Khuzama. On the same day they moved from Pfushumei to Kidima in the present-day Kohima district. The movement was fast and persistent. By 4 April, the Japanese forces were already in Viswema while a massive number of Japanese troops overwhelmed Kikruma. This was where the battle actually began. By evening the Japanese had sent an advance party to attack the Rajput and Assam regiment cantonment of the Allied forces at Chakabama. Another party was sent to break the Assam Rifles trenches that were stationed to defend Kohima. The swiftness with which the Japanese soldiers moved earned them some early victories. The simultaneous attack by the Japanese troops engaged the British army on all sides.[114]

Cannons were fired by the Japanese at the British storage at Sokhriezie, Kohima, from Phesama (the village near the present day Naga Heritage village which hosts the famous Hornbill festival of Nagaland). The Japanese also positioned their troops at Chedema and fired cannons at the DC bungalow which are said to have destroyed the cannons placed there. Details like the killing of two Sher Regiment soldiers near Kohima village by Capt. Kobayashi are still talked about by the old veterans. As the battle of Kohima started, the deputy commissioner, Charles Pawsey,[115] took shelter in the trenches made in the bungalow complex with the support and company of a Naga, Dobashi Mhiesizolie Chasie, as the other staff of Pawsey were absent. Intense firing of cannons and guns was exchanged between the Japanese and the Allied forces. The war entrenched the Japanese soldiers into the surrounding villages.

As the war began, there were casualties everywhere. From Kohima village to the famed tennis court, (imagine having a tennis court in Kohima in 1944 exactly where the actual battle was fought), the deputy commissioner's bungalow and the present-day

Raj Bhavan, Jail Road, Kuki Piquet and Kohima town. While fleeing the war sites, the inhabitants of nearby Naga villages and localities were dispersed in many directions. It was difficult to locate many of them even long after the war was over. The Nagas also took shelter in the trenches they dug. Working for the Allied forces, they soon became the target.

The Japanese in the meantime did everything they could to attack the Allied forces. To cut supply lines was a natural option and the Japanese managed to cut the water supply[116] and force a situation where the villagers ran short of ration. The British now lay surrounded and under tremendous pressure.

The Royal West Kent soldiers and the Allied forces, including the Assam Regiment, Assam Rifles, the Gurkha/Sher Regiment, put up a fierce fight but suffered a lot of casualties trying to protect the deputy commissioner's bungalow even as they were hemmed in by the Japanese. By 11 April 1944, the 2nd Division British soldiers reached Zubza and Jotsoma and established their headquarters there under Major Gen. M.L. John Grover, the man who would play the most instrumental role in the entire Battle of Kohima for the British. After establishing themselves, the 2nd Division started their counter offensive to reverse the early setbacks.

Dobashi Mhiesizolie Chasie was still trapped inside the trench alongside Pawsey. They had already spent an incredibly tense twelve days in the trenches. They did not hear the tanks rushing to their rescue. The tanks were deployed immediately in the defence of Thebegei, the tennis court and the Raj Bhavan area to ward off the attacking Japanese. The two of them were eventually rescued and sent off to the Shohuza general headquarters to rest before being transferred back to Dimapur. The ordeal Chasie had to undergo with Pawsey was excruciating. Never in his life had he ever encountered such a bleak twelve days of horror. He was thanking God and his fellow Nagas for the trenches dug. The Allied forces had to rescue Pawsey in any case. Just as quickly as

Pawsey was sent down to Dimapur, Eric Lambert took charge as DC and assisted Gen. Grover in the battlefield.

Meanwhile the family members of Chasie were worried to death about his safety. There were no reports of his whereabouts. Family members feared him dead as he was thrown into the midst of the bombings. He was brought back to Khonoma, his native village, only after the battle. When he came back home in a British vehicle, he saw all of Kohima burnt to ashes and with just one or two houses struggling to stand. Such was the death and destruction of the war.

Chasie's experience was just one of many. Some never came back to tell their tales. Those who survived reminisce about the deadliest of battles they have ever seen, not knowing that even those fighting the war considered the entire period the ghastliest of all wars. They would think of the period where people killed each other as if they were animals and went on to butcher each other for three months without a break, devastating the entire region. It brought immense hardships to the people in Naga areas. The Kohima Educational Trust has recorded and produced some of these stories from surviving Nagas of the Battle of Kohima. The Trust have made it available on their YouTube channel.

From nowhere, there were thousands of soldiers and tanks and cannons and aeroplanes overwhelming the local population. The Nagas experienced the behaviour of both the British and the Japanese forces during the intense fighting. True character is brought out from such trying moments, was what all Nagas who experienced the war say. Although the Nagas aided and supported the British in ways beyond their imagination, public memory of the British is generally tilted in favour of the Nagas. The British and the Allied forces generally toed the line of Lord Mountbatten in appreciating and acknowledging the critical role played by the Nagas in the victory.

While the British moved and attacked and operated, they saw many Naga villagers abandoning their homes and rushing for cover in the safety of the forest or their fields. They were even scared of resting in the temporary thatch shelters in the terraced paddy fields for fear of the Japanese. There is a particular incident narrated about the bombing of a Naga village by the British where eight innocent Naga villagers were killed and twenty-five others were injured. It was felt that the British bombing was unwarranted as there were no Japanese soldiers within twenty miles of the village. For the eighty-odd village homesteads and granaries destroyed, the British offered no compensation as was their practice in other areas during the war. Author Khrienuo[117] says this happened at a village near Tesangki.

The atrocities committed by the Japanese soldiers were excessive. The memories of those times are still recalled by villagers as they sit around their fireplaces. The tradition of oral storytelling serves as the right medium of telling and retelling the brutalities of the Japanese. Right from the time they reached the Naga Hills in present-day Nagaland, the Japanese forced many Nagas to work as porters. They would force the Nagas to carry their arms and ammunition, and make them walk on foot for days. There were no incentives offered by the Japanese except for the occasional offer of future help in return for a service rendered. If the Nagas disobeyed, the response was immediate execution by gunfire or by hanging.

However, it has also been recorded that the Japanese were not always like that.[118] When they first landed in Phek, they had even opened schools and provided books and other materials for the people. They taught the Japanese language to willing individuals. Those that did learn the language would later recite the alphabet to anyone who asked them. In Jakhama, the Japanese even visited the church and attempted to teach them the language besides some Japanese songs. The fact that both the Nagas and the Japanese were of mongoloid stock was repeatedly propagated by the Japanese soldiers to identify themselves with the Nagas based on a similar race. But the 'brothers and sisters' approach did not work once the Nagas got a rude awakening as the true colours of the Japanese soldiers slowly surfaced. The Nagas were benevolent hosts till such time as the Japanese troops started snatching away their rice, fowl and pigs. The uninvited guests had become the never-imagined oppressors. The theft or the acquisition by force left the Nagas disgusted. Their honour was desecrated right before their eyes. This was most unacceptable.

There was no recorded meeting of any village deciding to go against the Japanese. But the response to the humiliation inside their own kitchen was the tacit understanding of the Nagas to immediately lend any amount of support to the Allied forces was achieved, that too without making a fervent appeal. This was true of not just one village but of every Naga village, as they shared the same experience. The Nagas were ready to listen to the appeal of the soldiers of the Indian National Army. They promised to compensate for the food from the rations expected to arrive from Burma. As discussed previously, the Japanese soldiers started behaving badly against the Naga villages once their rations were short and this led to the uniform response of non-cooperation from the Nagas.

Thereafter the weapons and ammunition carried by the Nagas as forced labourers for the Japanese troops did not always reach the desired destination. To avoid the aerial bombings, they had to hide in the dense forests. It is said that during one such procession, the Nagas saw the British fighter plane approaching them and they threw away the arms and ammunition they were carrying and fled for safety in the jungle. The Japanese soldiers ran for cover too and in the melee, they lost the weapons. But it is told that many of these weapons were hidden by the Nagas and later handed over to the British. They were rewarded for weapons captured or stolen—it did not matter to the British as long as they were Japanese weapons. The only problem was that while the Nagas hid in the jungles, the Japanese managed to raid the villages to feed themselves by taking over the houses and the granaries. The Japanese were continuously in search of hideouts or safe places where they would not be detected by the warplanes.

15

The Story of the Greatest Battle Ever Fought

In 1944, Kotuku Sato, the commander of the Japanese 31st Division was a battle-hardened army commander. He had served in the Japanese Army since December 1913. In December 1942, when he took over the 31st Division with the rank of Lt Gen., he was on his way to Burma. Arthur Swinson, a British army officer who served in the 2nd British Division at Kohima, in his book *Kohima, The Story of the Greatest Battle ever fought*, writes the Indo–Burmese region was one of the 'wildest and toughest in the world'. Before advancing to Kohima and Imphal, the 31st Division of the Japanese had been allocated 3000 horses and 5000 oxen, the principal task of which was to carry ammunition and rations for the troops. The Japanese forces were given only as much rifle ammunition as they could carry, and food enough only for three weeks.

A highly trained soldier, Lt. Gen. Sato has been described as a person who was 'stubborn, one-track-minded, and painfully orthodox'. Whatever may be the truth of this, one fact is quite clear: he knew how to make his division get a move on, and commanded one of the most remarkable advances in military history'.[119] As Japanese troops poured over Chindwin, Sato was commanding a division in battle. His objective was to reach Kohima and he was expected to reach in fifteen days. And once he captured it, 'he could turn south and slaughter the British as they retreated. The name of his objective was 'Kohima'.

In the preface to his book, Arthur Swinson quotes Admiral Lord Mountbatten as stating that 'the battle of Kohima will probably go down as one of the greatest battles in history'. He states that the actual siege of Kohima was 'only fourteen days'.

Sato's superior and commander of the 15th Army, Lt General Renya Mutaguchi's headquarters was at Maymyo, some 220 miles south-east of Homalin, and twenty-five miles to the east of Mandalay. Mutaguchi's plan for the offensive, which had been arrived at after months of argument with Gen. Kawabe, commander of the Burma Area Army, and Imperial headquarters in Tokyo, was to attack the British in the Arakan (that is the coastal sector of Burma), then, when they had committed their reserves, to attack their forward base at Imphal. Things had not gone exactly to plan. The British divisions in the Arakan, attacked on 5 February, had not retreated as Mutaguchi had imagined they would, but stood and fought, relying on air-drops to replenish their supplies. On the night of 7 March, Lt General Yanagida's 33rd Division had attacked from the south towards Tiddim, and then, as the 17th Indian Division began retreating, cut the road behind it, and moved in. And now Yamauchi's 15th Division, and Sato's 31st Division were across the Chindwin, making a total of over 100,000 men, all trained, equipped, and burning with a fanatical desire for victory.

Arthur says that Mutaguchi dreamt of far greater conquest. He thought the politicians in India, particularly the members of the Congress party, were 'inciting'[120] the people as the Japanese army advanced towards Indian borders. He thought the whole Indian population would rise 'tearing the British Raj to pieces'.

Arthur captures the geography of Kohima in the manner of earlier British colonial explorers and here he writes:

'Kohima lies on a saddle connecting two mountain ridges, some 5000 feet up among the Naga Hills. To the south the green mountains roll upwards some 10,000 feet towards Mao Songsang, while to the north-west the ground drops away precipitously into a deep valley, pointing towards Dimapur. To the west the wooded slopes of the Aradura Spur run up towards Mount Puliebadze and Mount Japfu, 'dark, spectacular peaks which dominate the country for many miles'. To the east the land rises, hill after hill, towards Chedema and Jessami, then disappears into a wild untrodden region left bare on the map and marked simply 'dense mixed jungle'. The Naga Hills form the northern sector of the great mountain barrier between Burma and India.'[121]

Between 1942 and 1943, the Japanese generals lost precious time, dithering on whether to capture Imphal and Kohima by pursuing the British after their ouster from Burma. The 23rd Indian was the only division of the British empire in the north-east frontier of India protecting the buffer area from the Japanese attack. Within the Japanese high command in Tokyo, there was an active debate on capturing Imphal at the earliest since the British forces had already been chased out of Burma. The commanders in Burma decided to differ with Tokyo, giving Gen. Slim the much-needed space to reorganize his defence.

Mutaguchi can be credited with pushing the agenda of launching an offensive against the British forces at Kohima and Imphal in 1943. It is to be noted that he had officially rejected the idea in 1942 but having assessed the situation he changed his position in 1943 and urged the idea upon Gen. Kawabe, the Burma Area Army Commander. Also, he had now been given charge of the 15th Army in March 1943.

Another factor was Subhas Chandra Bose, commander of the renegade 'Indian National Army'.

Bose was 'confidently predicting that revolt was simmering just beneath the surface, and with one more British reverse nothing could stop it bursting into fury from Bombay to Calcutta, from Madras to Delhi. Mutaguchi believed him; and the High Command believed Mutaguchi'.[122]

Gen. Slim was ready for the offensive. He had already understood the plans of the Japanese Imperial Army. He summed up Mutaguchi's intentions as: '. . . first, to capture Imphal, and second, to break through to the Brahmaputra Valley so as to cut off the Northern front and disrupt the air supply to China. A Japanese regiment would, we foresaw, make for Kohima to cut the Imphal–Dimapur Line and threaten the Dimapur base. We calculated the offensive would begin about the 15th of March.'

Thus the greatest battle would begin with the intention of Gen. Mutaguchi to fulfil the will of the Emperor.

16

The Tin Containers and the Japanese Rupee

It is rumoured in the Naga villages that the Japanese passed through during their arduous journey to Kohima that a tall, bearded man wearing a round frame glass accompanied Lt Gen. Sato in his campaign. As Sato smoked while soaking in the huge tin container of a bathtub outside his residence in Kigwema, the tall, bearded man, who looked like he was from north India to the villagers, was chatting with him all the time. The secret visit of Bose has become part of the local folklore. During his reported stay at Kigwema, Viketu Kiso is said to have been his interpreter. Legends aver that Bose came and stationed at a village called Ruzaho, some 75 kilometres from Kohima, and stayed with an interpreter by the name of Poswuyi Swuro. At the time of their interview in 2017 they were both aged ninety-four and ninety-six years respectively and both claimed to have been interpreter for Bose at that time. Bose is known to have requested the Nagas to support the efforts of the Japanese soldiers. "Don't fear the Japanese soldiers. they have come to drive out the British. The Japanese are here for the Naga welfare and Indian welfare. If they do any harm, report immediately to the General."[123] The role of Bose in the Battle of Kohima was to support the Japanese in mobilisation of the people. Bose had formed the Indian National Army (INA) and was seen as a revolutionary by the British. The intelligence agencies of the Commonwealth saw Bose's INA as the 'Japanese Indian Force' for his collaboration with the Japanese. Gen. Mutaguchi saw Bose as a 'significant factor'[124] in the U-Go offensives. Operation U-Go offensives included a major attack deep within India, Calcutta and beyond. The Japanese intended to use the service of Bose to enter India although an outright invasion was not in the mind of the high command in Japan.[125]

By the time he arrived with his tired soldiers at Kigwema, Sato saw some of the villagers had already moved towards the forest in search of shelter from the war. There were vegetables to be bought from them and rations to be garnered, with or without the currency they carried. There are records which suggest that they carried money to buy food. The invading forces used what is called the Japanese Rupee, printed in Burma and issued by the Japanese government during the war. What has been called the Japanese rupee is the currency note issued by the Japanese government during the invasion of South-East Asia during World War II. The currency notes were used extensively by the Japanese military authority and for a while, they were used to replace the local currency used in territories captured by the invading troops.

The Japanese Rupee was issued when its troops occupied Burma (Myanmar) after 1942. The Japanese advanced to Mandalay (Burma) on 21 May 1942 and literally forced the British to retreat into territories located within the British-controlled side of India. Till the time of the Allied forces' campaign in 1944, Burma was ruled by the Japanese. In 1942, the Japanese-issued currency notes were introduced to Manipur and parts of Naga inhabited territories as they invaded these territories.

When the Japanese began capturing territories, its troops confiscated all currency notes in circulation in these territories. At the end of the Second World War, the same currency lost all value and those who possessed it discarded it or it was confiscated by the authorities. In Manipur, the British authorities were helped by volunteers of the Manipuri monarch and other organizations who supported the Allied forces as opposed to those who were hand-in-glove with the Japanese through the INA volunteers. Many in Manipur used to keep the same currency as wartime souvenirs after hiding it from those who were tasked with the responsibility of confiscating them. Now many of these notes can be found in both private and public museums as curated items.

Plenty of such printed currency was used in Manipur and Nagaland. Surviving veterans and those who participated in or saw the war had these currency notes in their possession. The invading Japanese, perhaps in their dream of successfully swaying the result of the war in their favour, wanted to overrun the monetary economy of western South-East Asia, including Burma, modern-day Myanmar. In Manipur, there were sections of people who helped the British authority burn thousands of these Japanese Rupees after a warning was notified.

There are few oral accounts left of how the Nagas reacted to the march of the Japanese. The bearded man who appeared at Kigwema and Ruzazho is still a mystery to many people. Whispers in the kitchen and around the paddy field mumble the name of Subhas Chandra Bose, INA supremo. Could it be so? The INA, under Bose, was definitely a part of this campaign but many fiercely stand by the truth of his visit. The whispers die but the legends remain. The bald, bearded man with round Gandhi frame spectacles had to keep his identity hidden for fear of being caught by the British. Or he simply did not want his presence known.

It should, however, be noted that there are government of India-endorsed publications that say that Subhas Chandra Bose was indeed in Nagaland.

A brochure issued by the ministry of tourism, New Delhi, called the 'Incredible India - Legacy of Freedom' noted the travel itinerary of Netaji Subhas Chandra Bose. It says that Netaji stayed at Ruzazho in Phek district of Nagaland. Named after two lakes, Ruzazho is a beautiful village surrounded by magnificent hills. During the INA campaign against the British in 1944, the government of India brochure stated that Netaji liberated the village and made it the operational base headquarters of the INA. Subhas Chandra Bose stayed for ten days in this village and over 1000 Naga youths reportedly joined him in the campaign against the British. 'The house in which Netaji lived and the wooden cot on which he slept during his stay in Nagaland are preserved at Ruzazho Village. The love and respect for Netaji are reflected in the local folklore and songs', says the brochure.

The Japanese obviously needed the help of the natives to reach Kohima. It may well have been a pact between the INA and the invading Japanese Army to assist them till Kohima and Imphal but it required the Nagas to be informed or mobilized. Stories have been told of Manipuris, Kukis and the Nagas joining forces with the INA to support the Japanese Imperial Army. It should be noted that there are rare documents in existence that compile the textually recorded oral narratives of the Nagas who had seen and interacted with Subhas Chandra Bose in some Naga villages.

In her book *World War II in Northeast India, A study of Imphal and Kohima Battles*, Khrienuo Ltu writes about the first impressions of the Nagas. The British accounts are plenty and all aspects of the Burma Campaign till Kohima and Imphal have been thoroughly researched and written by many scholars and journalists and even war veterans.

The British had already settled themselves in Kohima and the Naga Hills long before the Japanese, especially Gen. Mutaguchi, envisaged a campaign into India through Kohima. Charles Pawsey did a lot of spadework in terms of intelligence gathering and mobilizing the local Naga employees of the government of British India. Preparations were already underway in Kohima when Sato reached Homalin in present-day Myanmar to establish his headquarters. Khrienuo writes of the amazement with which Viswema villagers reacted when the Japanese arrived in the first week of April 1944.

'The whole forest is moving! So many of them have come,' shouted a villager.

'The whole forest came alive and there was not one spot that was still. Men poured out of the tree copses, from behind every rock and green plant, the Japanese soldiers with guns outthrust, they made a terrifying sight, and our hearts froze within us. They surged forward and even as we stood transfixed, they had reached the village.'

From the moment they entered the village, the shock and awe which the Japanese invoked in the villagers was to remain till the last. The house was rather small for a general, but he had chosen to stay in the southern side of the village, where he would plan the attacks on the British forces. The daring Kamikaze style blitzkrieg on the British army led to some initial success in his attack. The British had already expanded their tentacles over Myanmar and the South-East Asian region. Kohima was but a speck of dust compared to the Burma theatre. America and England had different agendas but faced a common threat in Japan. Britain had more to lose in this battle than America. But the geopolitical game was lost on the Nagas as it was not their war. Some Nagas had been to France in the First World War as part of the Labour Corps and had seen the devastation of such a war first hand. But it was in Europe and they themselves never imagined what it would be like to be at the heart of the fiercest battle in the history of His Majesty's war.

Sato's withdrawal ended a war for the Nagas which they did not start. For a change, there were no attacks on the British colonial administration by the headhunters. Rather, there was active participation of the Nagas in the war, siding with the British forces in the unlikeliest of partnerships. Nagas were utilized effectively as porters, spies, stretcher-bearers and they even dug trenches for the British forces. This was singularly responsible not just for the victory but for the number of lives saved in the battle. Intelligence gathering is critical to winning wars. It is a cliché to say that but it is still the main basis on which planning is done and decisions taken before and even during war. Both strategic intelligence and tactical intelligence enable leaders or nations to fight and win wars. For this, the source of information on the ground is the most vital agency. The British forces discovered that the Nagas could not only be used as interpreters (Dobashis) but as active spies and map-readers in the battlefield. They were able to locate places shown on the map with as much accuracy and enthusiasm as they carried the rations and arms and ammunition of the British soldiers on the battlefield. Not caring for their lives, they were as much fighters as the British soldiers. The glorification of the 2nd Division who fought against all odds is justified only in so much as the contributions of the Naga volunteers are recognized as equal partners. There are accounts of the service rendered by the Nagas during the battle which are condescendingly described by some British and American authors, perhaps not intentionally, but it does a great disservice to the sacrifices made by the Nagas. In terms of grading the multiple services rendered by the Nagas, the comment made by Fergal Keane in his book *Road of Bones* is an example of the relevance given by the British forces: 'The most important function of the Naga tribes was the intelligence gatherers. With the European V Force operatives dead, captured or in hiding, the RAF's aerial photography of limited value in the Jungle terrain, the Nagas provided the only reliable flow of intelligence to the 2nd Division on Japanese Movements around Kohima.[126]'

When the Japanese finally settled their contingent in Kigwema and started their offensives from there, it was a case of the enemy within. The Japanese soldiers moved early and only rested for a few hours, sometimes attacking the British bastions for days on end. In between, the negotiations for rations turned from trade to downright extortion. Within a short span of time and unbeknownst to them, the relations with their host village soured. Not that the host village invited the Japanese to their fold but the Japanese having stationed themselves there, it was a case of the proverbial 'all is fair in love and war'. Or rather all colonizing forces needed no invitation for occupying a place they could conquer by force.

From different villages, the British officers organized porters for their soldiers. In this Battle of Kohima between two Imperial giants of the day, Charles Pawsey's presence and authority was like the balming breeze of a haven for the British in many ways. When the refugees from Myanmar were coming in droves and crossing Kohima onwards to Dimapur in 1942, Charles Pawsey had already mobilized thousands of Naga volunteers to cater to the sickly, tired, and hungry refugees coming over from Myanmar. It was the consequence of the Japanese takeover of Myanmar, and it was a clear sign of what was to come. Till date, there is a locality in Dimapur called the Burma Camp, which is a name carried over from the colonial period when the refugees from Burma camped there waiting for transportation through the Dimapur Railway station to their hometowns. The experience that Pawsey gained during this harrowing period was priceless. The logistics of handling thousands of people in distress and organizing food and stay for the refugees and managing a people who they colonized was not an easy task. But the experience gained by Charles Pawsey definitely reinforced the preparedness of the British forces at Kohima. As many scholars have mentioned, the soldiers of 1944 were better trained, better armed and better supplied than 1942. The British and the Allied forces were not going to allow the Japanese to repeat the Burma experience. The transportation of the 2nd Division and the two Indian brigades was a challenge for them and yet with the support on the ground from the Nagas and in the air from the RAF was crucial for the victory against Sato's forces. The handling of the refugees from Myanmar gave Pawsey the trained manpower that he needed. If Sato had someone like Pawsey already warming up to the Nagas, he would have smashed through with his forces to Assam via Dimapur and fulfiled the Japanese dream of replacing the British in India. However, it was not to be.

The Japanese had two allies, one among them the Naga nationalist A.Z. Phizo who had worked with the 7000 troops of the INA, led by the charismatic Subhas Chandra Bose. But they were not based in Kohima or the Naga Hills at the moment of the attack. Although A.Z. Phizo was an Angami Naga from the famed Khonoma village known by the British for the Anglo-Khonoma battles, he did not have enough people in place or he had not mobilised the people for this invasion and hence his efforts and support were insufficient to gather the Nagas in support of the Japanese forces. The other was Subhas Chandra Bose who had assured them that the anti-colonial movement in India against the British would join the Japanese when they took over Assam and the north-eastern frontiers of the Indian sub-continent. The Japanese had met Phizo and his younger brother at Rangoon and assured them of 'Independence of Nagaland' in exchange for his support. This was before Phizo assumed the mantle of leadership of the Naga National Council (NNC) and much before his campaigns had real hold over the villages. The irony of history is that once the British left India, some of the former Deputy Commissioners and political agents of the British Raj started advocating their support for Phizo. Ultimately, as has been attested to by the British themselves, it was down to the intelligence gathered on the ground and supplied by the Nagas that tilted the battle in favour of the British. Despite the shortage of supplies and the ensuing starvation, dysentery, malaria and cholera, the Japanese had trudged on stubbornly.[127] Only when Sato decided that the war was no longer tenable, and he had to take a conscience call for the sake of his remaining troops, did they retreat. The British troops chased the retreating forces till Maram and secured a decisive victory over the Japanese. Little did they think about the significance of this battle then. But it changed the course of world history.

The British themselves had not imagined that Kohima would be their Waterloo. And the headhunters, massacred in thousands to establish this city on a hill called Kohima, became their most important ally in the war. The Naga side of the story is one of unending misery and courage at the same time. While this is a biography of how Kohima came to symbolise a people's history and identity from its inception till the present, it is also a story of how the hunted became the hunters' best friend.

The baskets woven by the coarse nimble hands of the Naga headhunters carried the ammunition, the rations and the medical supplies in the three months of blitzkrieg. The hands that tilled in the terrace fields and the jhum fields became the porters for the British Army. As mentioned earlier, the Nagas were also held to ransom by the Japanese Army and made to carry their ammunition and rations on their way to Kohima from Myanmar. The difference between the British and the Japanese in their dealings with the Nagas was the key. The steep terrain of the battlefield was daunting for the British soldiers and if not for the Nagas, who carried water on their head for them, brought down the wounded on stretchers, walked for hours without much rest, navigated the forest paths without a map, but still ensured that the service was rendered with diligence, things would have been different for the British.[128]

17

When Nagas Smoked Foreign Cigarettes

Of over seventy-one Naga villages which endured the steady and brazen invasion of the Japanese during the Battle of Kohima, remembrances of the horrible past have been few and disparate. Oral recalling of the contributions of the Nagas to the victory of the British are scant and the acknowledgment even less. Later day attempts by both the Japanese and the British seemed like afterthoughts to preserve their memories of 1944 rather than to acknowledge the Nagas. As stated earlier, the Nagas who went to France as part of the Labour corps returned home to share their experience. The Nagas who had served the British in various capacities were the first to share their stories with their descendants. And when the war came, they were the first to be mobilized to defend Kohima from the Japanese invasion.

The British forces moved aggressively to cut the supplies of the Japanese soldiers.[129] They knew from their Naga spies that Lt Gen. Sato was facing a shortage of food and his soldiers were facing the twin challenge of death from either starvation or the cannon balls of the enemy. The regular aerial supply of food ensured that the Allied forces and their Naga supporters were never short of food. The aircraft[130] were used to provide not only reinforcements but also to bomb the Japanese positions. General Slim assessed the situation in Kohima and Dimapur with a prescient sense of things to unfold. 'Within a week of the start of the Japanese offensive, it became clear that the situation in Kohima area was likely to be even more dangerous than that at Imphal. Not only were the enemy columns closing in on Kohima at much greater speed than I had expected, but they are obviously in much greater strength. We were not prepared for so heavy a thrust. Kohima with its rather scratch garrison and, what was worse, Dimapur with no garrison at all, were in deadly peril.'

The dependence on air supply for both communication and provision was critical in the war. From casualty evacuation to supplying cigarettes, the transport aircraft performed what is one of the most important roles in the war. In contrast, the Japanese used horses and mules for their transportation, which, of course, were no competition to the fighter aircraft of the Allied forces.[131] The British provided the Nagas with everything through these supplies. The British gave rice to the Nagas as their fields were bombed and the villagers could not go to farm as the fierce fighting prevented civilians from moving about freely. There was no shortage of supplies to support the Nagas who were working in different positions aiding the British forces. Every resource was used sparingly and to great effect.

The British sent a mind-boggling 40 million cigarettes to the battlefields in Kohima and Imphal. By the sheer numbers, cigarettes seem to have been the main item of demand for the soldiers. The First and the Second World War had seen cigarettes being rationed to soldiers to calm their nerves while in the trenches. The Nagas who went to France during the First World War saw cigarettes during their days as part of the Labour Corps. Tobacco as such was available in the wild. But not even in its wildest dreams would the theatre of war in the Naga hills expect to see 40 million cigarettes being dumped during the war. On the other hand, water was so scarce in Kohima that even taking a bath was prohibited.

Due to the sharing of food rations, American or foreign cigarettes were unintentionally introduced to the Nagas by the British during the war. With enough cigarettes to spare, the Nagas would be assured of steady supply once the habit of smoking developed. In the aftermath of the war, a huge number of arms, ammunition and bombs were scattered everywhere in the debris. Whereas a global war was fought to defend a patch of land, American cigarettes found a way into Kohima and found few takers amongst the Nagas. It definitely was the first time that Nagas were exposed to the use of factory-manufactured tobacco and the first time that American cigarettes found their way into the hands of the Nagas. The air supply of provisions also introduced some Nagas to canned food.

The bombs which failed to explode or those which rusted over the years were found by some villagers and, in one village, one such bomb shell is even used as the Church bell in a quaint reminder of a gory past and an ingenious utility. Since the end of the battle of Kohima in June 1944, the remains of the battle have been strewn over the entire Naga Hills. Rusted and unrecognizable from their original form, the remains of the war are used for various purposes as the finders deem fit. Some use them as church bells, others collect war objects to keep in the house or a small private museum at their homes. Unbeknownst to each other, all aficionados of the Battle of Kohima memorialize the pieces they find, almost instinctively, as if to capture for eternity a part of that war which transformed their history forever.

Some trace their roots to the battle which transformed the Nagas from headhunters into spectators of a different kind of war. Even most of the British forces had never flown in a plane before the war. It was so much more astounding for the Nagas to see giant winged birds flying over their villages and fields to drop food and ammunition, and it was an even more horrific sight to see the fighter aircrafts bomb the forests and the Japanese positions. It was a puff here and a puff there during the time in the trenches or while they took their rare rest as they carried the wounded on the stretchers. The use of 40 million cigarettes during the three months' battle is an amazing feat. While the Japanese were friendly in the beginning, even polite to a fault, they lacked air support and as their provisions dwindled, they became aggressive with the Naga villages and went on to confiscate food items and probably anything that a human could consume including edible herbs. It might have been a survival strategy which worked in Singapore and the Philippines, but it did not work in Kohima. Nor did Lt Gen. Sato believe in snatching food even though he was fighting the twin forces of the battle-hardened British soldiers and a severe shortage of food for his soldiers. In fact, in the end, the decision to withdraw was not due to the lack of courage but because the sustainability of the war depended on the supply of food, ammunition and reinforcement. It was the wrong time to add to the hostilities between the Nagas and the Japanese. As it were, the Nagas were fully rallying behind the Allied forces. The reasons may be simple, but their attachment to the British was instrumental in converting the headhunters into various service providers, the likes of which even the British had not imagined. Porters were always taken from the local populace. The British had made it part of their strategy since the early colonial days. Spying or acting as a scout was a natural, instinctive trait of the Nagas and therefore the Nagas required no training for that. But the way in which the service of the Nagas were used in this war was as if the entire strategy was already planned. Porters, spies, stretcher carriers, and even some as soldiers of the British army were part of what the British termed the V Force. The job descriptions were born out of necessity and the skill sets were beyond the expectations of the British. This made the force even more formidable. The Japanese had determination and a suicidal bravery which stood them in good stead in the first attack. It was as if the Nagas were tailor-made for these services. The British forces took full advantage of the headhunters. From the first siege of Kohima in 1890 to strengthening the Allied forces in the Battle of Kohima in 1944, a lot of water had flown under the bridge of colonial disdain.

After the battle ended in the defeat of the Japanese, the stench from the thousands of bodies piled up in Kohima down to the Imphal road, then known as the road of bones, engulfed entire villages in and around Kohima. A town of dead bodies, as it was remembered later by the populace, where the people searched for weapons and anything useful—it made scavenging a pastime of the survivors. For the Nagas suffered both at the hands of the Japanese and the British. Having participated in the war both as spectators and as the V force, the Nagas emerged from the battle as graduates of the new form of warfare where technology and superior weaponry was required to beat the enemies in addition to courage and skills. In an amazing exhibition of simplicity, most Naga survivors of the battle described the entire war experience innocently as 'having a good time with the British army.'[132]

Some of the Naga soldiers and the V Force were awarded gallantry medals by the British. Even today, the war veterans wear the British Empire Medal, the Burma Star and the 1939–45 Star, all with Certificates/Citations proudly. When Prince Andrew, the Duke of York, visited Nagaland in 2012 as part of the British Royal family's visit to the countries of the erstwhile realm and Commonwealth nations to mark the diamond jubilee of Queen Elizabeth II's coronation, he was the first member of the British Royal family to visit Nagaland in sixty-seven years since the Battle of Kohima. Quite innocently, the war veterans met him and put in a request to revise their pension from 500 rupees from the British government as it was not sufficient to sustain themselves. He left with an assurance, 'I will see what I can do.' A demand made to the Prince sixty-seven years after the Battle of Kohima is noteworthy for two reasons. The Prince mentioned in his tribute to the war heroes that the Queen remembers the sacrifice made by the Nagas and added that the past was well recognized and cherished but the future is more important. While the sacrifices were remembered by the Queen, the veterans were insistent on the raise in the pension they were receiving for the time spent fighting the Japanese together. They wanted to re-establish the link with none other than a member of the royal family. Some of the veterans questioned whether their role in the war they did not invite was worth it after all.

Generous accolades have been heaped upon the bravery and service of the Nagas by those who wrote memoirs or books on the battle of Kohima. However, to this day the role played by Charles Pawsey is nearly immortalised as if it was only him who fostered the relationship. The Nagas reciprocated in an honourable manner and the rest is history.

The cigarettes and the food enlivened the camaraderie during the three months of fierce fighting. The Labour Corps recalled sharing good food in plenty with the British soldiers as they went from one Japanese position to another, evacuating wounded soldiers and sometimes fighting along with the British army. Pork is an integral part of the Naga diet and pigs are reared in the villages by every family. The local pork reared in the backyard in a village home is a delicacy. When the Japanese ran out of supplies, they would simply snatch any pig they saw in the villages and take it by force to eat.

In the initial days, the Japanese paid for the vegetables and the food they bought from the Nagas. As their supply and provisions ran out and the war raged on, they started taking whatever food they could get by force. The Japanese pushed the Nagas right into the arms of the British. The British were well organized and dealt with the locals in a proper manner, as almost all the Nagas would testify. For every service rendered, they paid well and were never short of supplies to share. Many Nagas remember to this day that it was not just the simple sight of aircraft spraying bullets from their machine guns on the Japanese that both mesmerized and fascinated the Nagas, but it was also the sharing of supplies in times when food was scarce that rejected the theory of brotherhood based on race proposed by the Japanese. Veterans say that the war was won not just by the surplus of food available with the British but because the Allied forces could convert the best locally available human resource to their side.

18

Recruiting the Labour Corps

Christianity had already come to the Naga Hills by then. In 1942–43 the number of farmers tilling the fields and working for the harvest of new souls at the same time was growing. The mission was powered by the sayings of Jesus, 'The harvest is plentiful, but the labourers are few. Therefore pray earnestly to the Lord of the harvest to send out labourers into his harvest.' Charles Pawsey, the tall deputy commissioner of the Naga hills, rumoured to have an affair with a Naga woman besides fulfilling his obligatory duties to the British empire, was the recruiter-in-chief of the Nagas to the Labour Corps. In the end, he married a widow of a tea planter from Assam.

The recruitment of labourers from amongst the local population was not new. Although the administration had various other duties assigned to them, one of the unspoken responsibilities was to recruit labourers through coercion, agreements or even through wage payments. From the labourers at the tea gardens to the road constructions and finally as porters for the visits of the political officials, the British empire needed thousands of labourers. The British East India Company had already transported millions of workers from eastern and central India for their tea estates in Assam. The descendants of those workers are now an integral part of Assam with more political teeth than their ancestors and are referred to as the tea tribes by the Government of Assam, perhaps as a reminder of their past. Amongst them the communities having scheduled tribe status in other parts of India prefer to call themselves Adivasis.

The tea tribes are not a homogenous community. They belong to various tribes and some are backward-class Hindus. After Independence there has been a regular representation in the Union government from their community in the form of cabinet ministers or junior ministers. That has not been the story with the Nagas. The tea tribes were transported forcibly to colonial Assam in the later part of the nineteenth century in what is now known as the largest mass shifting of population during the colonial times in India. The total population of the tea tribes is estimated to be over 7 million today. From extremely harsh living conditions to low or unpaid wages, the labourers in the tea gardens of Assam were made to suffer like escaped convicts forced to work as slaves. Their conditions were often compared to the slaves in Africa and the harassment they received at the hands of the European managers was inhuman. Apparently, many of them ended up in the Tezpur lunatic asylum set up in Tezpur in 1876. It has since been renamed Lokpriya Gopinath Bordoloi Regional Institute of Mental Health. Lack of proper health care facilities added to the misery of the indentured labourers in the tea estates. From little or no wages in the nineteenth century under the British to the recurring debates in the twenty-first century on increasing wages, the history of forced labourers recruited to clear the vast forest tracks and develop the tea gardens of colonial Assam is one of exploitation and devastation.

Closer home in the Naga Hills, the recruitment was done for basic services to the British and not for large-scale economic interests. The first Naga Labour Corps recruited by the British empire was in 1917, and they were sent to France. From crossing seas and wearing uniforms to being the first Nagas to land in Europe thrilled the headhunters. It was the excitement of something bigger than what they had imagined was in store for them. The recruitment drives also made it clear that besides being paid, they would be exempted from any taxes that might encumber them. It was the same drill for those carrying loads of ammunition, digging trenches, rescuing wounded soldiers, and assisting in road building in the battle of Kohima. As records show, the conscription of the labourers was not always an easy transaction. The conscription included mobilization of corvee labour in areas where the empire had control over the territory. The forcible recruitment sometimes caused a lot of heartburn. But it was in the nature of the power relations between the subdued villages and the British. The call came and some volunteers took up the assignment. Some out of fear, while some out of adventurism, but when you were conscripted, your destiny was conjoined with whatever cause your employers were fighting for.

The Burma campaign had begun. Somewhere in the Arakan hills the Chindits had defeated the marauding Japanese forces, boosting the morale of the British Army and the Allied forces. But the Nagas weren't bothered about the Burma campaign or the Japanese troops. The able-bodied farmers, mostly new Christian converts serious about their newfound religion as much as their harvest, were being sought to join the Labour Corps. The deputy commissioner's office was requisitioning for two important events: a possible trip to Burma to assist the Allied forces and to take care of the refugees from Burma. It was a traumatic ordeal for both the refugees who had walked days and miles over the difficult terrain with hunger and fear as their companions in the long march to Kohima and for the Nagas who tend to the weak, and sickly and hungry, and addressing the never-ending flow of zombie-like humans into Kohima was a Herculean task. Some lived due to the caregivers' diligence, and some died for they were nearly dead upon arrival, and many did not reach Kohima as they perished in the bosom of the mighty hills. The headhunters became nurses in a day, answering to the call of the needy. This came to them easily. The service was given as required without any complaints. Perhaps this particular experience gave Charles Pawsey the idea of organizing the Nagas into a disciplined Labour Corps. He wasn't posted in the Naga Hills during the First World War when the Nagas were sent to France as Labour Corps. Although the Nagas who survived the First World War came back with a new understanding of warfare at a global scale, they were not able to share their experiences with the masses. Nor could they develop the Labour Corps into something permanent, a force of conscripted labourers paid in rupees.

The war would anyway displace thousands of villagers, and they were ready fodder for the kind of work that the Allied forces would need. Securing men from the surrounding Naga Hills was therefore not difficult for Pawsey. As mentioned earlier he was ready for the war much before the Japanese Imperial Army entered Homalin. He knew the Nagas would be approached to help the Japanese. The talks with Phizo in Rangoon had given hope to the Japanese for support from the Nagas. There was no way the Japanese could have anticipated the rapport built by Pawsey to yield a result detrimental to their agenda. Subhas Chandra Bose also promised the Japanese massive ground support without assessing the reality on the ground. These missteps did not deter the Japanese from entering the Naga Hills and the Imphal Valley.

There are myriad ways of understanding the way the recruitment was done. How Charles Pawsey pulled it off is now an effort hard to imagine, given the lack of modern technological facilities for both communication and networking.

Two stories illustrate the experiences of the Naga farmer who joined the Labour Corps in 1943.

19

Ralan: The Headhunters' Battlefield

The local missionary had tilled the land hard through spring and was expecting a good harvest for his family. A hardy farmer, he could walk miles for days traversing the scraggy hills, preaching from village to village to keep his flock together. He had always had a bountiful harvest in previous years, and he was content with his work as a farmer which sustained his missionary duties in the neighbouring churches. On the day he received a call from the deputy commissioner's office to join the Labour Corps, his wife was expecting their second child. It would be a baby girl. By the time he came back from the war, he would see the birth of his daughter—a baby born during the Burma mission. Although his village was in the Lotha country as the British would call it, it was just a day's walk to Kohima. Overall, five of them went to the war as Labour Corps from Ralan.

The local missionary was short in stature, but his companions and fellow villagers were of good height. They were told that their task would be to assist in rebuilding the bridges bombed by the Japanese in Burma. They were used to carrying sacks of rice from the field to their granaries. And it was not easy to trek the jungle tracts to reach the village. Without exception, all Naga villages were on a hilltop. That's where the headhunters had the vantage point and felt secure.

When they came back after a harrowing year, they would narrate their stories to anyone who saw the medals they received. They had settled in a place where their ancestors fought with the enemy to hunt heads. It was literally a jungle clearing where the village of 900 households responded to a challenge from the neighbouring villages. The Ahoms would develop cordial relations with this village as it was the closest Naga village to Sarupathar in Assam. It is said that the Ahom king would requisition the Naga warriors from this village for a fee. Besides the oral tradition of narrating the journey, there were no written records. The Burma star proudly displayed in their homes now is testimony to their participation in the Burma campaign as porters. Lest one assumes that the job of a Labour Corps member was only carrying loads of heavy machinery or materials, it must be emphasized here that the Labour Corps was in the thick of the battle, running for shelter when the bombs were lobbed towards them just as much as the Allied forces were. Sometimes they would go ahead to spy on the Japanese and prepare the Allied forces for what was coming.

There was amongst them a very timid farmer who would flee even at the slightest rustle of leaves, leaving behind everything he was carrying. He remembered only the cement bags he carried the entire journey. Crossing mountains higher than he ever thought he would see in his life at the foothills of Assam, he seldom took a break, but he welcomed the sudden attack by the Japanese army, as it allowed them to leave the load and scurry for shelter at the nearest crag or cave. The five of them joined the other recruits from across the Naga Hills at Kohima. From there they were dispatched to Burma.

When they returned home after the war, they found the life back home difficult to adjust to. Two of them took refuge in their missionary work. Immersing themselves in the ministry they dedicated their entire lives to preaching the gospel. The missionary was the only one who did not receive the Burma star. He got his wages of 40 rupees in 1943 and he was probably content with it. He didn't care much for the Burma star, a medal which had no significance in his life. He was after all a devout believer who would rather work for the harvest than a medal. Be that as it may, he narrated his ordeal with stoic forbearance. There was some confusion with regard to his batch and number. On their way back, his roll call was mixed up with some members from another district and his Burma star was lost in the confusion. However, he was least flustered, having collected the money promised on contract. Forty rupees was a substantial amount for a farmer in 1943, well worth the sacrifice to work in an unknown place, which his ancestors had journeyed from while migrating aeons ago to settle in the present location. He came back to the joys of seeing his second child and only daughter cry in the arms of his wife. That was a reward by itself, a joy to behold for all the travails of serving the empire.

They crossed the mighty Saramati mountains to reach Burma. They didn't remember the names of the villages they travelled to. There was no time to think of recording the journey. Rumours of a hailstorm of Japanese firearms made it impossible to keep a straight path. In the cover of the dark and with a heavy load of cement bags on their back, they moved stealthily towards the river, where a bridge was blown away by the Imperial Japanese Army. He didn't understand the meaning of the act nor the intention of the Japanese. He was busy obeying the orders of the commanding officer, a tall white man whose name he couldn't remember. They knew somehow that he was a missionary and had asked him to pray for the food on several occasions during the breaks. He prayed in Lotha and was happy with the fact that they had asked him to counsel his fellow Nagas. Long after he came back, he still wore the soldier boots issued to him in Kohima. Being used to walking barefoot all his life, this was something new. He would boast to his wife of how he had served in the Allied army, Labour Corps. He even learnt to fiddle with a gun from the British soldiers. He saw some British soldiers and some Nagas die during the journey to and from Burma. It was not an easy sight to behold for a missionary. He believed that all this would be over soon. They were the longest years of his life, and he lived till he was 104 years old. The war was not his, nor did he think much about it. The office of the deputy commissioner conveyed in unclear terms that the invasion by the Japanese Imperial forces would affect their village too. The headhunting days were over due to the conversion to Christianity. And they had to leave their ancestral village to start a new village for a very painful reason. New converts and the Animists could not stay in the same village due to conflict of religion between them. The social fabric had been ripped apart. The new settlement was referred to as the Canaan, in a biblical re-christening to represent the fertile land as the promised destination not yet revealed to them.

The reshaping of the global world order required only his ability to carry loads as a porter under the Assam Civil Porter Corps in the Burma campaign. He did not comprehend the impact of his role, paid as he was for his services. There was no mention of whether the amount paid was satisfactory. Just as he didn't bother much about the Burma Star he didn't receive, he was not ready to discuss the worth of payment of forty rupees for the next sixty years that he lived. He went back to his work with a new zeal, never looking back at the time he served the empire. For the other four who went along, the Burma Stars they brought back are still preserved with the ribbon intact in their personal collection. It has become memory of the honour and recognition of the war they were part of. Their names inscribed on the back of the stars are now proudly displayed by their grandchildren who would have never imagined that their grandfathers went to Burma. It is recorded that the 23rd division of the Chindits, known also as the forgotten Chindits, was stationed in Bokajan, Merapani and Mariani, to prevent the Japanese from marching north. Ralan was close to Bokajan and it was another route to march up to Kohima should that be required. This was not known to many people, and the villages around the route had no inkling whatsoever. Historians have not covered this aspect of the precursor to the Battle of Kohima extensively. Their success at the Arakan valley against the Japanese Imperial Army meant that they had been tasked for a special purpose in Kohima.

Memories have been shared and retold many times in front of many a fireplace; and after many trees have been cut for the firewood, the stories remain the same for every returnee of the Labour Corps. The recruitment was open and had no datelines for enrolment. Some responded to the experience with calm. Some were traumatized by the constant shelling during the job. They survived it all and later were called brave and courageous. It was not the same when the Japanese finally took Kohima in the first week of April 1944. There was a different sense of urgency, the need to survive a war. The five persons from Ralan had gone on a mission without fully assessing the dangers. It was a paid job as far as they were concerned. Over the years, their experience shaped their outlook on life in ways they would not express. They met often to discuss their journey together. It was only providence that brought them back home. The new recruits were different in that they were not in it for the wages alone. They also wanted to live and fight the enemies (not necessarily the Japanese) as much as they yearned to be united with their dispersed family members. For anyone who disrupted their normal lives with violence was an enemy. The enemy had no assigned names as they were from places they had never ever heard of or seen. There was Burma and then there was China far east of the Naga Hills. But to even think that the Japanese would one day descend on the Naga Hills and fight a bloody war was inconceivable to the Nagas. The white men from Europe and America were an inescapable reality then as they had visited and settled in the Naga Hills for more than a hundred years by then and didn't seem to be in a hurry to leave. And their stay cost so many lives that it was impossible to ignore. The violence perpetrated on the Nagas by the colonial force and their allies that led to the colonization of the Nagas and the consolidation of their rule was aided by the work of the missionaries through the schools and the churches they planted.

20

The Naga General: The Story of How the Samurai Surrendered to the Naga Dao

The sobriquet 'Naga General' was given much later when he joined hands with A.Z. Phizo to lead the nascent army of the Naga National Council. Unlike the missionary-farmer who participated in the Burma Campaign as part of the Labour Corps, the Naga General was born in 1918. While the contingent of porters was led by someone from the General's village older than he was, the missionary–farmer was born in 1901 at Moilan Village, a day's journey by foot from Phiro.

Phiro village is known as the first village to be established in the Lotha country, according to the Lotha Nagas. Phiro village already had the distinction of sending someone to take charge of the Labour Corps during the Burma Campaign. Gen. Yambamo Patton came from a village with so many of his peers in the Burma campaign already. The chatter in the village was about the number of fellow villagers who had left for the Burma campaign as porters. Not everyone got recruited to the Assam Regiment, raised first for the Burma campaign and then to fight the Imperial Japanese Army. The Assam Regiment was raised from amongst the various communities in the North-east, especially from what the colonial lords saw as an undivided Assam. It was befitting to see a warrior's descendant join the army for a new war for His Majesty's history. Shillong was the headquarter of this new force and the place where initial training was imparted there to the new recruits. He received from the army school a formal education, at the same time as he was trained to use the new weapons. It was a change from the dao and the spear he was familiar with. He was not short of courage from the day he joined the service.

And he also descended directly from the founders of the village. It would seem he had the lineage and the legacy in his favour already. Destiny was to offer him something bigger. It was a time when schools were a far cry in the village. Education was to be sought some days away from Phiro and probably the best option was to learn how to till the field and hunt in the forest when time permitted. And so it was only after he joined the newly established 1st Battalion of the Assam Regiment at the young age of twenty-one that he joined the army school and passed the second standard while in service. In 1939, he joined as a sepoy. The promotion came steadily. From a Lance Naik to Naik took some time as that upgrade came with some patience. His first experience at the Burma campaign secured him that position. From then on, he was stationed in Kohima as the 1st Assam Regiment was tasked with the defence of Kohima in 1944.

If you travel through Kohima town today, the Assam Rifles headquarters is at the centre of the town, as it were, and the citizens of Kohima know it for, among other things, the canteen where the public visits frequently, and the helipad where VVIPs from the Centre land their helicopters whenever they visit. Or at least that's what the townsfolk think. Hardly anyone would think of this location as the camp where the 504 'C' COY was placed during the second siege of Kohima, to which Lance Naik Yambamo belonged. For the longest time till the Indira Gandhi Stadium was built in Meriema, en route to Wokha, the Kohima Local Ground, as it was called, was the only public ground which hosted every major event in Nagaland. When Jawaharlal Nehru, the first Prime Minister of India, visited Kohima along with Burmese Premier U. Nuh in March 1953, they gathered at the Kohima Local ground to have a public meeting. The Kohima Local ground had hosted two very important leaders of Asia and it was here on that fateful visit that the Nagas gave the cold shoulder to these two important leaders for being denied an opportunity to meet them and submit a representation on behalf of the Nagas. It was to show their resentment towards Nehru, and not towards U. Nuh. After his return to Delhi, Nehru adopted a very hostile policy towards the Nagas and sent in the army to quell the Naga rebels. That brutal chapter has already been recorded by many writers from the North-east and other parts of India as Nehru's failure to deal with a situation peacefully.

It was behind this fateful place that Yambamo Lotha and his company were encamped to stop the Japanese forces from capturing the DC bungalow and the headquarters on the Kohima ridge. He was a fighter, and waiting for the right moment was not his style. On the night of 13 April 1944, he decided to climb up the slope and spy on the Japanese forces camped right inside the Kohima Local ground. Celebrations were on in the Japanese camp. Temporary setbacks were forgotten because of the initial successes. They just had to take a small patch of land to secure Kohima. It was a Herculean task, however. What seemed like a near victory a few days away was stretching into months. The merrymaking was unusual for a force in the thick of a fierce battle. More than a month into the battle, the nerves of the Japanese soldiers must have been steeled to action, their zeal and spirits still intact as much as Lt Gen. Sato would have wanted them to possess. For Yambamo, it was intuitive as a warrior to have the clarity to seize the moment. The headhunter's instinct rose to show its face. He didn't expect the Japanese soldiers to react in fear when others adopted their strategy of attacking the enemy with shouts of war cries. But when he did attack with his stentorian voice exerted to the utmost, the booming shout shocked the Japanese soldiers, catching them by surprise as they ran helter-skelter for their life, leaving behind the food, drinks and even their weapons as they searched for shelter. The war cry had its intended effect. Even today the shrill Naga war cry can be intimidating and formidable, with the listeners only feeling secure and safe because it is a demonstration for cultural performances rather than an actual warning before an attack. Without a second thought or concern for his own life, he steadied his hands with the weapon his forefathers trusted the most, the irreplaceable dao, and chased the retreating Japanese soldiers. He slayed them with the swing of his strong arms, taking the Japanese heads whenever he caught them as they ran, reliving the moments of his forefathers whose spirits lived through him, blood soaking his hands as it dripped from the dao after every kill. Such bravery and courage were unseen and unheard of by his comrades in the regiment. Eventually he would lose count of the heads he took that night, recalling later of having taken either seventy-eight or eighty-seven heads in just one attack.

The war was on an even keel at that point of time and this turned the tide for the Allied forces, as the Japanese saw the ferocity of the native entrapped in a war not their own. They had seen Nagas support or be in service of the empire, but they never anticipated that the Naga attack would be so devastating, not only to their well-trained, determined soldiers, but also to their fighting spirit. The Japanese, for all their initial successes in Kohima, would see a change in their fate after this attack by one Naga matching the mighty Japanese samurai. An uneven battle, a decision on the spur of the moment, the indomitable Naga instinct carried by the headhunter's descendent, blew the momentum towards the British empire, making His Majesty's interests safe and making the Americans heave a huge sigh of relief. Lord Mountbatten and Gen. Stillwell would now mount more attacks on the Japanese forces as the advantage given by this single man's act of valour had unmistakably tilted the war in their favour. His superiors basked in the glory of his heroics, and the 1st Assam Regiment was recognized as the best fighting regiment of the British Indian Army. The hero was not from the UK or America, he was the best of the headhunters from Phiro village of the Lotha country. But the honours were equally shared by the regiment and its officers. There is no account of whether his officers were sleeping when he single-handedly launched the attack. They might as well have been because he did not bother to go back and seek support from his company. He attacked alone and shared the glory with his regiment.

Gen. Yambamo took a voluntary pension after the war. He was given the Gallantry Award of Military Medal besides the Burma Star, distinguished service medal and the colonial times Indian Independence award for his unmatched bravery in the battle. He was offered a promotion, for that was the only service honour the empire could bestow to a non-British fighter in their service. Like a true Naga headhunter, he refused the promotion, citing the reason that as the only son he had to take care of his ailing parents and thereby availing the option of taking voluntary retirement. He was given pension for his service and long after he died in 1956, his wife, who not only survived him but still lives, is enjoying the pension. It is another story that he was killed at the hands of the Indian Army at the young age of thirty-nine, after he joined hands with the Naga leader A.Z. Phizo.[133] The irony is that it was the Bihar Regiment which killed him at Nrung Longidang Village in Wokha District. Enraged by the fact that the Bihar Regiment had committed the sacrilege of camping inside the church at Longidang Village, he decided to attack them and was killed in the process.

History has adequately recorded the mighty Allied forces defeating the Japanese Imperial Army. During the Burma campaign, Gen. Wingate emerged as the hero leading the Chindits. For the Nagas, and the Lotha Nagas in particular, Gen. Yambamo was no less a figure than Gen. Wingate. Save for World War II aficionados, hardly any discussion on Gen. Wingate occurs today, but the Nagas remember the forgotten hero Yambamo for his courage and for displaying the true spirit of the Naga headhunter who fought His Majesty's battle and was one of the critical factors on the ground for the beginning of the Japanese retreat from Kohima. But his story would not be told by the victors who distributed the medals. He made it to the

London Gazette as a war hero, a mention in the footnotes of the empire's history. He was without any expectations and that was his greatness.

For all we know, his story is remarkable in that the victory he secured that fateful night changed world history as far as the Nagas are concerned. The hands had to be treated with salt and hot water to remove the blood which had caked on them at the end of his fight. The blood had welded his hand to the Dao, and it was difficult to remove. That attachment to the Dao with the blood of the Japanese soldiers remained with him in his memories. His ancestors must have experienced the same for the remedy was local and readily available. His courage embodied the Naga spirit. And for all men and women who participated in a horrifying war for His Majesty's empire, the majority displayed nothing but courage and fortitude in the face of a determined force.

Whether it was the missionary-farmer who served as a porter, or the many who served as foot soldiers in the British Indian Army, the story of their involvement exhibited the same spirit as the protagonist of the two stories above. A history of the Battle of Kohima is incomplete without the stories of heroes like Gen. Yambamo from Nagaland. Reams of papers would be required if we were to record the involvement, experience and the lessons of every Naga who was embroiled in the Battle of Kohima. Village after village will tell you stories of the tepid response of the British after the war. They will narrate how Gen. Sato came and left dejected, not knowing how he was fighting his own inner battle in a political, military and career-long rivalry with Mutaguchi, leading to the disastrous defeat of the Japanese Imperial Army whose tragic fate was sealed right here at Kohima. For they will not remember Gen. Yambamo who single-handedly beat them at their own game in the Kohima Local ground. For he was the only Naga to have hunted Japanese heads at a time when hunting heads was a dying practice since the arrival of the American missionaries and of their overarching influence over Naga culture. And it was not just one head of the Japanese warriors. The Samurai surrendered to the Naga Dao.

Timeline of the British Expeditions to the Naga Hills

1. 1832–33, first British expeditions:
   - In January 1832 Captains Jenkins and Pemberton lead 700 Manipuri troops with 800 coolies from the Manipur valley and fight their way through the Naga hills as they travel from Manipur to Assam. Cachar is formally annexed to the British territory on 14 August 1832.
   - In 1833 Raja Gambhir Singh, accompanied by the Manipur Levy under Lieutenant Gordon, marches through to Assam by a route a few miles to the east of Jenkins's track.
2. 1835
   - The British East India Company invites the Manipur state and Tularam of North Cachar to occupy or control the hostile Nagas in the Naga Hills. Tularam protests the offer. Manipur sets up a post at Semkhor for a short time accepting the offer.
3. 1837
   - Francis Jenkins, now commissioner of Assam, places a European officer to a post near the Naga 'country' to endeavour to bring the Naga chiefs to terms with the British. However, the expectation of fresh war with Burma prevent his actual deputation for a time.
4. 1838
   - The Court of Directors of the EIC approves the raising of a small Cachari Levy to deal with the 'Naga Difficulty'.

The entire tract of North Cachar is transferred to Assam and attached to the district of Nowgong.

5. 1839

- E.R. Grange, sub-assistant at Nowgong, is chosen to conduct the first Angami expedition. On his first visit to the Naga hills, he finds a way to Assam via Samaguting, where he established a permanent military post. Grange is given permission to establish a market at this post.

- Grange is authorized to subdue all the Angamis north of the water-pent, and the Manipur King is invited to subdue all those south of it by Francis Jenkins, commissioner of Assam.

6. 1840

- Grange launches his second expedition in January 1840 expecting the Manipur Levy to meet him halfway but finds that they had turned back without waiting for him. The expedition results in the burning of five villages and the capture of eleven Naga prisoners.

7. 1841

- Prisoners are released after the Naga chiefs enter into a written agreement with Grange.

- Principal assistant in charge of Nowgong, Lieutenant Bigge is authorized to visit all the villages in the Naga hills. He carries out his tour without any opposition. The Dhansari River is fixed as the boundary between the British districts and the Angami tracts. A depot for salt is also agreed upon, to be opened at Dimapur. The British convey to the Angami villages to stop the slave traffic being carried out with the Bengalis of Sylhet.

- The attempt to make a road to Samaguting fails.

8. 1842–43

- An agreement is made to pay yearly tribute to the authorities at Nowgong and the Angami chiefs promise to stop internecine feuds.

9. 1844

- When Eld, an assistant, is sent up to collect the first yearly tribute, the chiefs defy him and absolutely refuse to pay. This is followed by a series of daring raids, in one of which they overpower a Shan outpost and kill most of the sepoys.

10. 1845

- Captain Butler, principal assistant of Nowgong, is deputed to the Naga hills with a strong force. He manages to secure a tribute of ivory, cloth and spears from the Naga chiefs. But the raids do not stop.

11. 1846–47

- Captain Butlers's second expedition leads to the same agreements as the previous year, although they would not be honoured. The only change is the establishment of a permanent market at Samaguting, a new stockade and grain godowns at Dimapur and a road from Mohung Dijooa to Samaguting.
- Sezawal Bhogchand is put in charge of the stockade. He would be killed in an ambush in 1849.

12. 1849

- Lieutenant Vincent's first expedition does not succeed, as the officer falls ill and has to retreat. The Nagas celebrate the retreat by launching a series of raids all around the border. The policy of the British government changes from mild interference to aggressive expeditions in view of Bhogchand's murder.

13. 1850

- Lieutenant Vincent returns to the hills in early March to carry out the second expedition. He burns down half of Khonoma and establishes a stockade at Mezomah and remains there to carry out punitive actions against the Naga Villages around Mezomah.
- Upon subsequent mobilization of the Nagas against him, Major Jenkins orders a strong force with guns to

rescue Vincent. This is the tenth Naga expedition of the British, wherein they capture one fort and Khonoma, and the troops are eventually withdrawn in 1851, failing to subdue the other villages.

14. 1851–52
   - Following the invasion in 1850 by the British, the Nagas raid no fewer than twenty-two times in North Cachar, in which fifty-five persons are killed, ten wounded and 113 taken captive by the Nagas.
   - Captain Butler recommends to the president in council for full withdrawal of the British troops from the hills and non-interference in the internal feuds of the Angami villages. A warning is also issued to the Raja of Manipur to desist from aiding and abetting the feuding Naga villages.

15. 1853
   - A European officer is appointed to check the Nagas from North Cachar.

16. 1854
   - A Manipuri force invades the Angami Hills, without British intervention, as the persistence in policy of non-interference in the Naga hills was in place.
   - The policy of settling the Kukis as buffers in between the Naga hills and North Cachar is mooted as a response to the raids by the Court of Directors. The enlistment of Angamis in the military police is also mooted as a solution but it failed, as of the thirty-seven Angamis recruited none could last in service for even eight months.

17. 1862
   - Lieutenant Governor Sir Cecil Beadon reviews the policy of non-interference. He orders the immediate opening of communication with the Nagas by an officer subordinate to the commissioner. The then officer of North Cachar, Lieutenant Gregory, supports the call for review.

18. 1866
   - Lieutenant Gregory occupies Samaguting with a force of 150 police, all hillmen and well armed. The Government of India bans the Manipuris from carrying out any retaliatory expeditions into the Naga hills. All outrages committed by the Angamis in Manipur are to be taken in concert with Lt Gregory.
   - Razepemah village is razed to the ground by Lt Gregory. In retaliation men from Razepemah raid the village of Sergamcha and butcher twenty-six Mikirs. Lt Gregory levels Razepemah to the ground as a punitive action.
   - The first school and dispensary are opened at Samaguting.

19. 1867
   - Manipur rejects the boundary laid down by the British.
   - Mezoma and Khonoma villages submit a complaint against the Manipuris for their attempts to levy contributions.

20. 1869–70
   - Captain Butler, the then deputy commissioner of the Hills District, and Dr Brown, the political agent at Manipur, meet to trace out the boundary lines between Manipur and the Naga Hills. A boundary commission is appointed.

21. 1872
   - In July 1872, the boundary issue is settled around the statement that the line of 1842 should be maintained in all essential points as it was clearly identified.

22. 1874
   - In 1874 the Naga hills are made over to the charge of the newly appointed chief commissioner of Assam.
   - Major Godwin-Austen is deputed to explore the boundary up to the Patkai Pass.

23. 1875
   - 3 January 1875: Captain Butler reaches Wokha, a large village on the western slope of the Wokha 'Peak'.

For the murder of one coolie, Captain Butler retaliates by destroying the village and killing forty Lothas.

- The chief commissioner Colonel Keatinge suggests the change of policy to political occupation of the hills and shifts the headquarters from Samaguting to Wokha while maintaining Samaguting as an outpost.
- Captain Butler is killed in an ambush at Pangti. Lieutenant Woodthorpe burns Pangti village in retaliation.

24. 1877–78

- The British Government decides to acquire effective control and influence over the Naga hills and therefore proposes to shift the headquarters from Wokha.
- On 6 December 1877 the political officer Mr Carnegy, embarks on an expedition with a force commanded by Captain Brydon consisting of 196 rank and file of the 42nd Assam Light Infantry and fifty police.
- Additional reinforcement of troops is consequently deemed necessary, and 100 men from the 43rd Assam Light Infantry, under the command of Lieutenant McGregor, are requisitioned. This new dispatch includes the inspector general of police, Captain Williamson.
- The political officer Carnegy dies due to an accidental shot by one of his sentries. Captain Williamson assumes temporary charge of the political officer's duties.
- Kohima is occupied on 14 November 1878 as the new headquarters of the British Empire in the Naga hills.

Timeline of the Battle of Kohima, 1944

1. January
   - Japan activates operation U-Go.
2. 8–16 March
   - The Japanese 15th Army moves its troops across the Chindwin River towards Imphal and Kohima.
3. 22–26 March
   - 50th (Indian) Brigade under Brigadier Hope-Thompsom is attacked by the Japanese forces of the 31st Division at Shangshak.
   - General William Slim starts the formation of a force to counter the invading Japanese Army.
   - 50th Parachute Brigade withdraws from Shangshak.
4. 28–29 March
   - 17th Division fights with 23rd Division at Jessami.
   - Japanese Air Force attacks Imphal and cuts the road between Dimapur and Imphal.
5. 30 March
   - Royal West Kents march to Kohima.
   - After the attack on the 1st Assam Regiment's positions at Jessami and Kharasom, the battalion retreats to Kohima and Dimapur.
6. 4 April
   - Lt General Sato's 31st Division attacks Kohima, specifically the GPT ridge.

7. 5 April
    - The Japanese troops flood Kohima Village.
8. 6 April
    - The siege of Kohima begins.
9. 5–20 April
    - British troops start the defence of Kohima.
    - The 2nd British Division relieves the Kohima Garrison.
    - Kohima siege turns into a fierce battle.
10. 13 May
    - 31st Division is driven out of Kohima as the Kohima Ridge is cleared.
11. 25 May
    - General Sato writes to the 15th Army HQ about his decision to withdraw from Kohima
12. 31 May
    - 31st Division is ordered to leave Kohima.
13. 2 June
    - The Gurkhas recapture Kohima village.
14. 6 June
    - The final Japanese positions in Kohima are abandoned.
15. 22 June
    - The Imphal Road is reopened.
16. 5 July
    - Major General Grover is relieved of his command.
17. 7 July
    - Lt General K. Sato is relieved of his command.
18. 8 July
    - Mutaguchi orders general retreat.

Acknowledgements

The journey of this story began with several trips to the various locations mentioned in the book over the two years that it took to research and write.

From Sato's quarters in Kigwema, where my colleague and friend Medo Yhokha showed me the various haunts of the Japanese soldiers, to a trip to the Doyang Hydro Electric Project near Pangti village in Wokha district, where I saw the exact site where Captain Butler was speared—I travelled to various places, and a lot of people regaled me with stories of the glorious history of the Nagas during the colonial period.

Among all my trips to the famous green village of Khonoma (I made several trips there), the best and most informative one was with Premanka Goswami and his lovely family. We got the privilege of having Viketuno Hiekha from the village enthral us with stories of their great ancestors. Ms Hiekha also assisted me in my research.

My editors, Premanka and Rea Mukherjee, have been extremely helpful in offering valuable support throughout.

From the very beginning, over tonnes of conversations, Peter Modoli, head of marketing, Penguin India, had encouraged me to bring this unknown chapter of colonial history to light, and I am very grateful to him for that.

Due to my political commitments, it was not easy to afford one space where all the writing could be done, but I was lucky enough to have many people offering me their support when I needed it.

My friend Larsing Ming Sawyan provided the much-needed space in Guwahati and Shillong. The White Owl in Dimapur opened at the right time for me—I had the best writing space in their library. Thanks to Nimrei Phazang and Yanmi Phazang for the continuous supply of good food while I was in Delhi. All of them have been a blessing in the long and arduous process of writing this book.

I thank Dhiren Sadokpam for the assistance in the research, for his expert comments on the manuscript and for being available any time of the day for a long discussion on the writing.

A mention must be made here of my intern, Hachamo Patton, from G.D. Goenka University. Thank you for your assistance.

Finally, thanks to Pao and the kids, for all their patience and understanding during my long absence.

Notes

1   The Kohima district is primarily inhabited by the Angami tribe, and the forest belonged to the present-day Kohima Village, known also as one of the largest villages in Asia.

2   When this story started King William IV (William Henry) was King of Great Britain and Ireland and King of Hanover from 1830 until his death in 1837. King George VI was the King of the United Kingdom from 1936 to 1952. In comparison the Showa Emperor Hirohito was the longest-ruling monarch in Japan's history and reigned from 1926 until his death in 1989.

3   As early as 29 July 1940 Emperor Hirohito had summoned his chiefs and vice chiefs of staff to the palace to question them about prospects for war with the United States. As quoted in the book *Hirohito and the making of Modern Japan* by Herbert P. Bix (p. 376), Hirohito asked if they were 'planning to occupy points in India, Australia and New Zealand'. By April 1942 the Japanese had captured strategic points in the remote Andaman and Nicobar Islands, territory belonging to British India (p. 446, Bix). Bix further writes, 'On January 7, 1944, he (Hirohito) sanctioned an offensive from Burma into Assam Province, India. The aim was to pre-empt an Allied drive to recover Burma and possibly bring about an uprising of Indian nationalists against British rule. Although no documents indicate that Hirohito himself actively promoted this particular offensive, it was just the sort of operation he had pushed for all through the war—aggressive and

short-sighted. The Imphal campaign, justified partly to defend Burma and partly to restore troop morale, began on March 8 and bogged down in early April.' (p. 474.) B.H. Liddle Hart, in his seminal work, *A History of the Second World War* writes, 'The object of the "Japanese" offensive was to foil an allied offensive in the dry mountain passes from Assam - not to attempt a far-reaching invasion of India, or "a march on Delhi".' (p. 658) It (The Arakan Offensive) also led General Mutaguchi, commander of the Japanese 15th Army, to recognize that he could not regard the Chindwin as a secure barrier, and that to forestall a British counteroffensive he would have to continue his own advance, thereby leading to the Japanese advance across the India frontier in 1944, and the crucial battle of (Kohima and) Imphal. (p. 458.) From Emperor Hirohito's assessment of the war and the advances made to India it is clear that the ultimate aim of the Japanese offensive would be to enter the British held Indian subcontinent.

5 Authors such as Martin Dougherty and Jonathan Ritter have referred to the battle as the 'Stalingrad of the east'. There are other similar references by other authors. 'For Kohima was to Burma what Stalingrad was to Russia and Alamein to the Desert.' (p. 7, C.E. Lucas Philips, *Springboard to Victory: The Burma Campaign and the Battle for Kohima*).

6 https://web.archive.org/web/20131225171213/http://www.nam.ac.uk/exhibitions/online-exhibitions/britains-greatest-battles.

7 At midnight on 31 May 1944, Sato had ordered his troops to withdraw from Kohima due to 'the exhaustion of rationing ammunitions'. 'British—too many guns, tanks and troops. Japanese going but back in six months.' This was scrawled on a wall in Mao by a Japanese soldier who knew some English. Cited in the book *Imphal* by Lt Gen. Sir Geoffrey Evans and Antony Brett James (p. 321). Lt Gen. Sato had sent a terse signal to the Burma Area Army Headquarters:

'The tactical ability of the 15th Army Staff lies below that of cadets. This statement is recalled by the villagers when his troops retreated from the villages they had occupied. There is no written record as such.

8 *The Burma Road* by Donovan Webster, p. 255.

9 As quoted in Verrier Elwin's *Nagas in the Nineteenth Century* (pp. 112–183). Read also 'The Last Angami Rebellion' (p. 40–42) in the *Gazetteer of India Nagaland Kohima District*, 1970. Alexander Mackenzie's book titled *History of the Relations of the Government with the Hill Tribes of the Northeast Frontier of Bengal* was published in 1884, much earlier than the aforementioned book by Verrier Elwin. In his preface he states that 'the Assam Proceedings' referred to 'those reported by that Administration to the Foreign Office of the Government of India. (p. IV) The British policy was very succinct. After various discussions and proposals by the Political Agents, the Assam Proceedings, March 1878, clearly notified the decision.' (p. 132)

10 'The first attempts to open up the Naga territory were made rather in the interests of Manipur than India, and were due to the fact that Rajah Gambhir Singh was desirous of strengthening his hands against Burma, by intimate trade relations with Assam, and it was thought well to encourage him in this Policy.' *Pioneer*, 24 March 1870. Mackenzie wrote this in an article titled 'The Naga Hills'. Mackenzie specifically mentions the interest Gambhir Singh had for the Naga Hills as per the Political Proceedings on 19 December 1833, Nos. 85–93. 'Facts came to light which made it clear that the object which Gumbheer Singh had in view was the permanent conquest of the Naga Hills. The ambitious Manipuri would have been a very dangerous neighbor for our vassal Purunder Singh, whom we were then endeavouring to establish on the throne of Upper Assam, and the Government began to feel uncomfortable in prospect of Gumbheer Singh's operations.

It did not absolutely prohibit him from subjugating the Nagas; but it forbade him to descend into the plains on the Assam side.' (pp. 101–102).

11 *Being Mizo* by Joy Pachuau, p. 87.

12 *On the Edge of Empire*, edited by David R. Syiemlieh, pp. 44–46. Sir Robert Reid, Governor of Assam from 1937–42, in his note on the future of the presently excluded, partially excluded and the Tribal Areas of Assam puts forth the demarcation as, 'For purposes of the Constitution Act, 1935, these areas, in terms of the Government of India (Excluded and Partially Excluded Areas) order, 1936, are:- Excluded Areas- The North-east Frontier (Sadiya, Balipara and Lakhimpur) Tracts. The Naga Hills District. The Lushai Hills District. The North Cachar Hills Subdivision of the Cachar District. Partially Excluded Areas- The Garo Hills District. The Mikir Hills (in the Nowgong and Sibsagar Distritcs). The British portion of the Khasi and Jantia Hills District, other than the Shillong Municipality and cantonment.'

Categorizing them as Backward tracts, he reviewed the migration from 1837 to 1941 from Sylhet and the Bengal district of Mymensingh to Assam Valley. He writes, 'The census of 1941 showed a Mussalman population in the Assam Valley of 1,304,827. In 1901 it was 2,48,842. In 40 years, therefore, it has multiplied itself by very nearly six times. This unceasing invasion from Bengal is clearly bound ultimately to have a substantial effect on the relations between the plains and the still Mongolian hills and to separate their interests more and more widely as time goes on . . . Under the heading "Recommendations" at pages 99–101 of the "Memoranda" prepared for the Indian Statutory Commission in July 1928, the Government of Assam gave their opinion as to the future of the Backward tracts as follows:- 40. For these reasons the Government of Assam are convinced that in the interests both of the Backward tracts and of the rest of the province the present artificial union should be ended. The Backward

Tracts should be excluded from the Province of Assam and be administered by the Governor-in-Council, as Agent for the Governor-General in Council, and at the cost of Central revenues.' The reason I quote this is because Governor Reid extensively dwells on this aspect of migration from Bengal into the Assam Valley in the context of the geopolitics of the region where the 'problems arising out of the Sino-Japanese war and the world war of 1939, have underlined the importance of the North-East Frontier in relation to Tibet, China, Burma and Japan.' This and the changing demographics factored in the prolonged discussions about the future of the excluded and partially excluded areas. So it was not just the decision to classify as excluded and partially excluded areas but to estimate the constitutional future of the unadministered areas which sat at the back of the British Empire as they accumulated more regions in *their quest for control* of the Naga Hills.

13 'The late nineteenth century speeches of British imperialists provided clearer insights into the colonial motives in introducing Christianity in her colonies.' Kumar Ghoshal, People in the Colonies, pp. 30–31. As quoted in *British Policy and Administration in Nagaland 1881–1947*, p. 68. He writes further, 'Obviously, the introduction of Christianity and imperialist expansionist policy went hand in hand. ON the other hand, the machineries of colonialism such as Christianity, education and other natural byproducts of colonial administration assumed the role of white man's burden in civilizing the backward people. as a corollary, as elsewhere British motive in the introduction of Christianity in Naga Hills, inevitably, formed a part of their policy of territorial expansion.' Ibid., pp. 68–69. Not only grant in aids to missionary efforts, but the British Government also provided the much-needed security for missionary work. 'The saying that in the expansion of British colonialism the Bible follows the flag became evident when in 1886, Rev Rivenburg, while giving report of the Kohima mission

field said: 'The presence of a regiment of infantry and five hundred armed police indicated that the day of peace was at hand and of all points among the Nagas this appeared the most favourable of missionary labor.' Piketo, p. 69. Schools and institutions opened by the missionary had the colonial administrators sanction because it made communication easier for him.

'The main purpose of the schools were looked upon as evangelistic as the missionaries so often stated in reply to those in America who objected to their educational activities.' F. Downs, p. 95, as quoted in Piketo.

Sajal Nag analyses the relation between imperialism and Missionaries by citing a Congo conference of European states held in Berlin in 1885. 'The conference was attended by almost all European colonial powers. The mutual binding between missions and colonial politics was at its strongest where the two accepted the "white man's burden" as a "genuine responsibility", which some anti-imperialist missionaries referred to as Christian imperialism. The theory of operational unity was put in such a way to so as to give the impression that colonialism and Christian missionary endeavour were two sides if the same coin. Certainly, there were common fields of operation. Education and medical works were the areas in which missionaries and colonial structures were mostly integrated.' Sajal Nag, *The Uprising, Colonial State, Christian Missionaries, and Anti-Slavery Movement in Northeast India, 1908–1954*, OUP, 2016.

A more detailed and lengthy discussion on the relationship between Christian Missions and the Empire is discussed in the book *Missions and Empire*, edited by Norman Etherington, OUP, 2005.

14 This is an oft-repeated story told to the many visitors to Khonoma Village. It has been declared as India's first Green

Village and along with the visit to the forest conservation sites tourist are treated to their proud history and culture.

'The name given to the village is not infrequently ascribed to some local feature. Thus Kwunoma (Khonoma) are the men of the "Kwuno" trees, a large number of which are said to have been cleared from the site selected when the village was first built.' *The Angami Nagas* by J.H. Hutton (p. 43), OUP, 1969.

15 In *Defeat into Victory, Battling Japan in Burma and India, 1942–1945*, Field-Marshall Viscount William Slim says: 'Our own build-up was proceeding rapidly. The concentration of the 2nd British Division was practically complete—too complete as far as its transport was concerned, for its lorries, parked nose to tail, threatened to turn the two-way main road into a one-way track. An attack by twelve Oscars on a mass of this useless transport, jammed into a village, lent point to my exhortations to 33 Corps to get it out of the area. Luckily the R.A.F. maintained such a degree of air superiority that we did not pay the heavy penalty that should have been exacted. Relieved of this excessive transport, the division found, like others in Burma, that it could move faster and more freely without it. The leading brigade (33) of the 7th Indian Division had arrived, also by air, from the Arakan fighting, and 23 Chindit Brigade was already advancing in several columns south-east from the railway. One of these columns had its first serious and successful brush with the enemy on the 16th April. On the 22nd it attacked a strongly held village but was repulsed. Within the next few days, in co-operation with a well-directed air strike, it again attacked, and this time took the village. Stopford, commanding 33 Corps, whose headquarters was established at Jorhat, was rightly urging the 2nd Division to advance, but the terrain and the type of warfare were new to British troops, while the unavoidable

arrival of the division piecemeal made the task of Grover, the
divisional commander, a difficult one.' Pp. 420–421.

'As it was impossible in the hills to build any landing
strips, the 5th Division became completely dependent on air
dropping for all its requirements. It also relied for direct fire
support largely on the fighter bombers of 221 Group, R.A.F.
What this regular air supply and support meant in skill and
strain to the aircrews only those who have flown among these
shrouded hills can judge. Yet throughout the whole of this
monsoon the fighters of Air Marshal Vincent's 221 Group
flew over our troops every single day. I do not think such
devotion has ever been surpassed in any air force, and I doubt
if it has been equalled.' P. 470.

16 The author had visited Kigwema village to see the house in
which Sato camped, a picture of which is shown in the book.
Mention may be made of the scribblings on the wall of a red
house where it is written, 'Japanese troops arrived at Kigwema
on 4.4.44 at 3 P.M. during world war II.' A gentleman from
the village stays there with his family in the house in which Lt.
Gen Sato stayed. They had done some minor repairs, but the
main structure of the house stands as it was then.

17 https://censusindia.gov.in/census.website/data/
population-finder
    Dr Radhakhrishnan, the second President of India,
inaugurated Nagaland state on 1 December 1963. *Gazetteer of
India*, Nagaland, Kohima District, p. 55.

18 The Preamble of the Constitution of Kohima Village Council
reads, 'Kohima is the land of Kewhimia of Angami Naga Tribe.
Kohima village is one of the largest village in Asia. The village
is believed to be 700 years old. There are four Khels namely,
Pfuchatsumia, Dapfutsumia, Lhisemia and Tsutuonomia.
The early settlers of the village came from various directions
at different times. However, all of them belong to the same
Tenyimia family and many of them are even found to be from

the same family lineage. Hence, it is difficult to make a strict division of people on the basis of Clans within the village as all members are found to be related in one way or the other. The name Kohima was given by the British when they first arrived at Kohima as they could not pronounce Kewhimia properly. Kohima was therefore derived from the name Kewhimia. There are different versions regarding the origin of the name "Kewhimia". However the most popular version was derived from "themia kekra upfhu uwhi vor keta" meaning many people started visiting the village after it was established. Originally the early settlers was called Pfutsana (Animists) as they considered Heaven and Earth as Father and Mother and in times of distress, they called out to God as "Teikiju Apfu APfu".' Constitution of Kohima Village Council.

19   The Khels of the Nagas are different from the administrative Khels of the Ahom Kingdom. J.P. Mills's description of the meaning of 'khels' for the Lotha Nagas is illustrative.

'Every Village, except the small ones, is divided into two or more "khels". Sometimes, but by no means always, a little strip pf open ground marks the division between "khels". IN some villages these 'khels' mark the division of clans. But this is not common. Usually a "khel" appears to be nothing more than a convenient division of a village in which men of various clans live. Sometimes some feature of the site gives the "khel" its name, e.g. Hayili ("level") khel in Akuk. Sometimes, as in the Wokhayakho ("Wokha men's khel") in Pangti, the first inhabitants have given a name to the "khel". Usually a man lives and dies in the "khel" in which his forefathers lived and died before him. But he is perfectly free to go to another "khel" if he wants to.' *The Lotha Nagas* by J.P. Mills, Macmillan and Co. Limited, London, 1922, p. 24.

A more elaborate explanation is given by Dr George Watt on the subject of 'Khel' among the Angami Nagas in a paper presented before the Royal Anthropological Institute in

London in 1887. 'The Khel system by which their village are split into rival communities does not however appear to have been fully understood. Instead of the sub-clans occupying different districts they are dispersed throughout the country, each village consisting of two or more of these sub-clans or Khels. It is no unusual state of affairs to find Khel A of one village at war with Khel B of another while not at war with Khel B of his own village. The Khels are often completely separated by great walls, the people on either side living within a few yards of each other yet having no dealings whatever. Each Khel maybe described as a small republic. The club system for the youths of the village prevails, each Khel having its own club house of dosta-khana, in which not merely young men, but also the young women all live together instead of with their parents.' pp. 463–464, *Nagas in the Nineteenth Century*, Verrier Elwin, OUP 1969.

For more on Khels in Colonial Assam, see Bodhittsava Kar, *The Birth of the Ryot, Rethinking the Agrarian in British Assam*, pp. 39–45, and the book *Landscape, Culture and Belonging, Writing the history of Northeast India*, edited by Neeladri Bhattachcarya and Joy L.K. Pachuau, Cambridge University Press, 2019.

20 'From Phitson (Kezhakhenoma), the Lothas continued migration towards Mao, Southern Angami area then to Khayima. Kha meaning Counting, YIma meaning puzzle or confuse, in other words, on counting they could not get the exact number of people because of the great population.'

Page viii, *The Lothas: In the Age of the Awakening* by T. Kikon 1993.

21 Akho Yhoka, *Tracing My Roots*, p. 60.

22 *The Angami Nagas under Colonial Rule* by K.S. Zetsuvi, 2014, pp. 17–18. Another version of the same matter by author Akho Yokha in Zetsuvi's book uses the word 'Robbers' instead of 'thief'. I quote, 'However, in spite of all the different versions

and interpretations, we are inclined to think that Angami is a term derived from the Zeliang word "Hangamai" which means robbers. It is told that the Zeliang Nagas who lived next to the Angamis, used to call them so because they were being ribbed and harassed by the Angamis and particularly the Khonoma people, which continued till the advent of the British. Moreover, the Angamis used to carry out raids on the plains of Assam. Therefore, it is quite possible that the British wanted to know this group of people from the Zeliang who were living near the plains.' Zetsuvi further refers to Hutton and Ursula Graham Bower's work. 'Hutton must have realised this fact when he said that it was very difficult on his part to understand the customs of the Kacha Nagaas (Zemis) as a result of their domination by the people of Khononma- J H Hutton, op. cit. p 16. In this connection Bower also mentioned that, The warlike Angami Nagas, who had come to power since the Naga migration, raided the Zemi constantly and exacted tributes.' Ursula Graham Bower, *Naga Path*, London, 1950, p. 44.

23 'The Zeliangrong came at a later wave of migration, constituted of Zemi, Liangmai and Rongmei allied to the Kabui Naga tribe who came by the Barail southwardly route; hordes of the first immigrants are said to have traversed through the impassable mountain region along the Barak in avoiding conflicts with the other tribes and ensconced in the western mountain tracts where they made home. Probably they came in search of brines. Only this tribe came along, not having joined the other body of migration. Yet the many powerful Zeliangrong villages are said to have an admixed Zeliangrong- Angami parentage. Eeven Razaphema is said to contain Zeliang strain in its original background. These Nagas were known as Kacha during the early British advent which in Angami Ketsa means deep forests, hence Kacha after Ketsa, the word used for a place.' P. 19, *Gazetteer of India*, Nagaland, Kohima.

24 https://thohepou.wordpress.com/category/tenyimi-naga/

25   Several books exist on the violence of the East India Company
     or the British empire's military missions into their colonies.
     I want to start with a quote from John Stuart Mill, the English
     philosopher and politician. 'Despotism is a legitimate mode
     of government in dealing with barbarians provided the end
     be their improvement, and the means justified by actually
     effecting the end.' J.S. Mill, *On Liberty*, page 236.

     The Harvard historian Caroline Elkins expounds on this
     in her voluminous book *Legacy of Violence: A History of the
     British Empire*. 'If Britain's civilising mission was reformist
     in its claim,' she writes, 'it was brutal nonetheless. Violence
     was not just the British Empire's midwife, it was endemic to
     the structures and systems of British rule. It was not just an
     occasional means to liberal imperialism's end; it was a means
     and an end for as long as the British Empire remained alive.
     Without it, Britain could not have maintained its sovereign
     claims to its colonies. Indeed, how could it have been
     otherwise?' P. 13.

     'By the nineteenth century, British global expansion and
     imperialism—or the extension of economic and political
     control over foreign lands through either informal or formal
     means—was a defining feature. In search of markets for its
     goods and capital, Britain preferred to keep the doors of free
     trade and investment open through informal mechanisms like
     treaties and the sheer force of its economic dominance. When
     necessary, however, it would annex a territory and exert formal
     political control, achieving economic supremacy through
     protectionist policies, which included tariffs, monopolies, and
     an accumulation of sterling reserves through a positive trade
     balance.' P. 9.

     Elkins describes vividly the process of colonial violence.
     'Violence enacted on bodies, minds, souls, cultures, landscapes,
     communities, and histories was intimately connected to the
     civilising mission's development dogma.' P. 15. 'Such violence

included corporal punishments, deportations, detentions without trial, forced migrations, killings, sexual assaults, tortures, and accompanying psychological terror, humiliation, and loss.' Page 16, Elkins.

These are the general overview of the violence that the British Empire took to its colonies. Sven Beckert in his book *Empire of Cotton* describes the emergence of global capitalism as a combination of states with merchant and settler ventures, but that only weakly asserted their sovereignty over the places and peoples in distant territories. 'Instead, private capitalist, often organised in chartered companies (such as the British East India Company) asserted sovereignty over land and people, and structured connections to local rulers. Heavily armed privateering capitalists became the symbol of this new world of European domination, as their canon-filled boats and their soldier-traders, armed private militias, and settlers captured land and labour and blew competitors, quite literally, out of the water.' Page 37.

Briefly tracing the characteristics of colonialism, the abovementioned scholars have highlighted the inherent and inalienable organs of colonialism, features of which are visible in the EIC and the British Empire's venture into the north-eastern part of India.

'After the war with Burma in 1824-26, the East India company (EIC) increased its military and administrative presence in Assam and the territories east of Sylhet. Officers and surveyors were restyled as superintends and commissioners. In the following decade they took steps to form a support structure to revive trade in the larger region. This primarily involved bureaucratic consolidation west of the mountain range separating EIC territories from the Burmese, and further eastward expansion by means of expeditions.' Page 80, *Founding an Empire on India's North-eastern Frontiers 1790–1840*, Gunnel Cederlof, 2014.

David Ludden quotes scholars on the primacy of resource and revenue in the colonial expansion and conquest. 'Amalendu Guha has begun the historical study of the basin's modern territorial appropriation by describing Assam's resource value for British capital in the nineteenth century., when armies of British India fought to conquer Burma, pacify the highlands, and thus accomplish what David Harvey calls a "spatial fix", to make this unruly space a profitable territory for investors. At first, during the fifty years of conquest and consolidation, the main concern was Company Revenue, and Assam fitted cheaply into Bengal.' *Landscape, Culture and Belonging, Writing the History of Northeast India*, edited by Neeladri Bhattachcarya and Joy L.K. Pachuau, Cambridge University Press, 2019, page 35.

26 S.E. Pearl, *The Nagas and Neighbouring Tribes*, 1874, Vol. 3, pp. 476–81.

27 Two important events determined this arrangement- one was the formation of the Manipur levy and the other was the signing of two treaties in 1833 and 1934 between the British Government and Manipur. 'In early times occasional communications passed between the British Government and the Manipur state, but our present relations may be said to have originated in the first Burma war. Manipur had been devastated by the Burmese, and its ruling family had fled to Cachar. In 1923 the British Government opened communications with Gumbheer Singh, one of the members of the Manipur family; upon which 500 Manipuris under his command were taken into the pay of the British Govenrment, and co-operated with the British troops in driving the Burmese out of Cachar. In 1825 this force was increased to 2000 men, and placed under the command of Captain Grant; it was denominated the Manipur Levy, and was paid, accoutred and supplied with ammunition by the British Government. Subsequently by the Ava Treaty of 1826, Gumbheer Sing was recognized as the Rajah of Manipur, though without any corresponding

obligation so far as the British Government was concerned.' Page 150, Alexander Mackenzie, *History of the Relations of the Government with the Hill Tribes of the Northeast Frontier of Bengal*.

28 Captain Vetch in his report on his visit to the Singpho and Naga Frontier as quoted on page 94 of Elwin's *Nagas in the Nineteenth Century* appraises the weapons used by the Nagas rather disparagingly. 'The arms used by the Nagas are the spear, dao, and occasionally a crossbow and arrows of pointed bamboo. The spear is thrown, and a rush then made with either to recover the spear or to carry off the head oj any enemy they may have fallen. They have no firearms and are greatly afraid of them.'

On the other hand the British army had superior firearms which stood them in good stead during their conquest. Just to give a small example, in the report by Moffatt Mills on the Military expeditions to the Angami Naga hills.

'Captain Reid of the Artillery, and Lieut. Bivar of the Light Infantry, with a detachment of the Light Infantry and two 3-pounder guns, proceeded to Mozumah in November and in December collected 600 coolies and dispatched rice and two mortars in progress ot Mozumah, which we reached on the 7th of December, after a harassing march of 40 miles from Deemapoor, greatly impeded by difficulties we experienced in getting the mortars conveyed over the hills.' Page 137, Elwin.

29 A detailed exposition has been given in the footnotes above.

30 *Founding an Empire on India's North-Eastern Frontiers 1790–1840* by Gunnel Cederlof, page 194.

31 Ibid.

32 *Nagas in the Nineteenth Century*, edited by Verrier Elwin, is a fine collection of all the British reports on their travels and ethnographic studies on the Nagas in the nineteenth century.

On the Edge of the Empire is a collection of key plans regarding the fate of the North-east by key British administrators at the end of British rule. Edited by David R. Syiemlieh.

33 *Nagas in the Nineteenth Century*, p. 114.

34 The following letter by Pemberton to P.C. Swinton, Chief Secretary to the Government, highlights the permission granted for the survey in the form of a military expedition: 'Anxious as we were to depart toward Assam we were however detained at Munipore until the 7th of January, before which date the Rajah had not been able to complete his arrangements for the prosecution of this part of our journey. His highness had very judiciously determined on increasing our escort from the two companies, which we ourselves thought sufficient in our letter of the 8th August last to your address, to the strength of 700 muskets, on learning that we were likely to encounter opposition, chiefly the benevolent hope of overawing the Nagas form fruitless resistance by the display of considerable force, and partly from his anxiety to place the safety of the British officers confided as he conceived to his charge beyond the possibility of danger.' As quoted on page 78 of Gordon P. Means, *Tribal Transformation: The Early History of the Naga Hills*, 2013.

35 Pages 94, 104–7, 204, 286, 290, 345–6, 391, 487, 538, 541, 546, *Nagas in the Nineteenth Century*, Elwin.

36 *On Being a Naga, Essays*, Temsula Ao, 2014, page 16.

37 Ibid., pages 17–20.

38 *Nagas in the Nineteenth Century*, Elwin, page 287.

39 Hutton, in *The Angami Nagas*, writes that, 'It is agreed by all Angamis, as well as by the other Nagas, that head-taking was essential to marriage in so far that a buck who had taken no head, and could not wear the warrior's dress at festivals, not only found it exceedingly difficult to get any girl with pretensions to good looks or to self-respect to marry him, but was help up to ridicule by all the girls of his clan.' Page 165.

40 Page 290, Elwin.

41 'To kill somebody of an alien village and to take his head means to gain his sol-stuff and add it to his own village's reserve of

magical power . . . only in the head and there in the parts around the eyes and in the lower jaw the best soul-qualities are concentrated. If there is a famine or an epidemic one believes that the magical power of the village has weakened and the warriors in consequence set out to fortify it by bringing in a head.' Page 341, *Imagining the Nagas*, Alban Von Stockhausen, 2014, Vienna, Arnoldsche Art Publishers, Stuttgart.

42 https://www.indiatoday.in/magazine/indiascope/story/19900915-as-two-tribes-in-nagaland-go-head-hunting-government-seeks-armys-help-to-maintain-peace-813007-1990-09-14
https://youtu.be/3hlhvGmDSAM

43 John Butler, *A Sketch of Assam*, 1847, pages 158–64.

44 'It was only many years later that the anthropologist Rodney Needham generally criticised the explanatory arguments made for head-hunting and showed that the existence of the belief in a soul-matter; could, on many cases, not be proved and had emerged rather from the imagination of the very early ethnographers and handed down in literature.' As quoted on Page 341, *Imagining the Nagas*, Alban Von Stockhausen, 2014, Vienna, Arnoldsche Art Publishers, Stuttgart.

45 There is the theory that head-hunting may have originally evolved from cannibalism. For more on this see https://kashgar.com.au/blogs/tribal-culture/the-practice-of-headhunting

46 I measure this from the date of the first expedition of the British military in 1832 till the shifting of the headquarters of the Naga Hills to Kohima in 1878.

47 'The Treaty of Yandabo had the effect of a sledgehammer on Burma's economy.' Page 71, Gunnel.

48 Page 68, Cederlof, *Founding an Empire on India's North-Eastern Frontiers, 1790–1840*.

49 Ibid., pages 170–71.

50 Thant Myint U., *The Making of Modern Burma*, pages 233–234.

51 In addition to that the British officials made disparaging and contemptuous remarks about the Assamese Princes. 'The Assamese princes were, however, mere worthless debauchees, and the security of our eastern districts made it necessary to retain strong military control of this part of the frontier.' Pages 2–5, Alexander Mackenzie, *History of the Relations of the Government with the Hill Tribes of the Northeast Frontier of Bengal.*

52 'Judging by reports from outside Manipur, this power hub was always described as aggressive, brutal, and torn by court disputes within the Meitei Royal dynasty. But the correspondence emanating from within the Kingdom projects a dramatically different image. Inside the hub, Burma could play its politics and pressure Manipur into submission. Likewise, the EIC manoeuvred between the members of the royal house to find a strong ally who would oust the Burmese from the hills. during the war, it was not self-evident which of the sons of Raja Bhagya Chandra would get the best of the situation. The EIC officers first planned on pensioning off the princes in Sylhet to prevent them from again invading Cachar. For a time, at loss as to how to control north Cachar, the political agent in Manipur favoured making the region over to Gambhir Singh to farm for twenty years. But the officers in charge of Cachar refused, having witnessed his brutal methods of suppressing people in the areas he conquered. Soon, however, the company found it most expedient to support this "bold and aspiring soldier" and make him a useful ally in Manipur. Supplied with arms and ammunition, Gambhir Singh recruited his soldiers among Manipuris, with the aim of being reinstated as Raja.' Page 196, Gunnel Cederlof, *Founding an Empire on India's North-Eastern Frontiers 1790–1840.*

53 'It was under the circumstances reviewed in the foregoing minute that two treaties were concluded with the Manipur state, namely, one of 1833 and one of 1834. By the Treaty

of 1833, the British government agreed to give to the Rajah of Manipur the line of Jeree River and the western bend of the Barah as a boundary; the Rajah, in return, agreeing to the following conditions, which are still in force.' Page 151, Alexander Mackenzie, *History of the Relations of the Government with the Hill tribes of the North-East Frontier of Bengal.*

54 Report on survey operations, 1872–73, Page 82, as quoted on page 11, Elwin.

55 Page 115, *Nagas in the Nineteenth Century*, Elwin.

56 The proposal to exchange the Kabaw Valley came as a surprise. But it was the offer of exchange that perhaps settled his mind. '. . . in 1833, two new boundaries resulted from the survey expeditions and negotiations with Ava. Both had a military-strategic significance, but only from the EIC's point of view, not Manipur's. First, the boundary between Manipur and Burma was shifted westwards and the Kabaw valley was transferred to Burma. This decision had been preceded by a tug of war between the two states at the expense of people of Sumjok, who strategically allied themselves with either Ava or Manipur crossing the river to reside on the eastern or western bank depending on the situation, Second , Manipur's western boundary was altered to include all lands upto the Jiri River in the lower hills, which ran south and discharged into the Barak. The decision was equally deliberate, intended to make Gambhir Singh responsible for preventing Naga attacks on villages in north Cachar. The Raja's initial response was to completely reject the prospect of losing the Kabaw valley, on account of the 'humiliation and shame he felt in agreeing to cede to the hereditary oppressors of his country a part of the territories of his ancestors' and the 'anxiety, apprehension and alarm the near neighbourhood of the Burmese would be certain to give rise to amongst the inhabitants of Munneepore. However, the boundary was a fait accompli and he yielded. The British

explained that, together with an annual payment to Manipur, the boundary at the Jiri was "compensation" for the loss of Kabaw, yet eight conditions were attached to the agreement with Gambhir Singh.' Pages 196, 200, Gunnel Cederlof.

57 *History of Manipur (Pre-Colonial Period)*, p. 339, Gangmumei Kamei.

58 Pages 150–151, Mackenzie.

59 'A village is, however, far from being a united community, as might have been expected. The unit of the Naga society is not the village, but the khel, called by the Angamis themselves "tepfu" or "tino". Many of these exist in each village. In Kohima there are seven different sub-divisions. These khels are endogamous sub-divisions. The members of each "khel" are supposed to be descended from a common ancestor, whose name the khel bears.' A.W. Davis, in Census of India, 1891, vol. 1, page 237.

60 David Scott was also the first civil servant to introduce the idea of seeking the assistance of Christian Missionaries for the hills.

61 *Manipur and the Naga Hills* by Major General Sir James Johnstone, pages 88–93.

62 Ibid., p. 192.

63 R.G. Woodthorpe, 'Extract from the Narrative Report', General Report of the Topographical Surveys, 1875, pp. 53–6, in *The Nagas in the Nineteenth Century* edited by Verrier Elwin.

64 *The Angami Nagas*, pages 17 and 367.

65 R.G. Woodthorpe, 'Extract from the Narrative Report', General Report of the Topographical Surveys, 1875.

66 John Butler, 'Rough notes on the Angami Nagas', JAS, 1875, Vol. 44, No. 4, *The Nagas in the Nineteenth Century*, Verrier Elwin.

67 In the Prologue titled, 'The New Musket', of the book *The Siege of Delhi*, Amarpal Singh writes of the Enfield Pattern 1853 rifle musket (p. 1853). 'The Enfield Pattern 1853

rifle-musket was a fine weapon. The single-shot, muzzle loading, percussion-lock firearm with a rifled bore didn't look particularly different from the earlier smoothbore musket (P1842) it was replacing in the armies of the east India companies. The difference in performance, however, was revolutionary, and the advantages of the new Enfield rifle quickly became obvious. The old musket had an effective range of not much more than 100 yards, with a maximum range around double that distance. The new rifle, in contrast, had a range of 600 to 900 years. Being rifled, the Enfield was inherently much more accurate. The weapon was deadly, too. Its conical Miniè ball ammunition had a higher velocity and mass, sufficient to shatter bone, unlike the round ball. It quickly became apparent that a cavalry charge against infantry manned with this new weapon would be an almost hpeless endeavour. The old tactic of forming hollow squares would become redundant as cavalry could be dispatched with ease thanks to the firepower of this new rifle. The user of the new weapon naturally held a huge advantage over a rival handling an older musket.' Page XV.

Gambhir Singh was apparently given 3000 muskets after the formation of the Manipur Levy. But the new Enfield Pattern came only in the second half of the nineteenth century.

68 'The British lacked the ability or skill to enter the hill tracts and win a war. Their troops were trained to fight in the open plains, not in the hills or forests.' P. 190, Gunnel.

'. . . the expeditions resorted to by the native states (Manipur and Tularam's country) to punish the outrages of the Naga seem to be accompanied with gross barbarities, and to involve the innocent and guilty, in one indiscriminate plan of murder, arson and rapine . . . such expeditions not only do not effectually stop, but seem to increase the plundering habits of their unfortunate victims. In proof of the correctness

of this opinion, I have only to refer to the fruitless efforts of
the detachment sent by the Munnipore state last year, and to
the assertion of Captain Jenkins, that the late incursion of the
Nagas into Cachar probably swung from a desire to avenge
the sufferings they endured from the Munnipore detachment.'
P. 195, Gunnel.

69 Historically used to define a native soldier or local
militiaman in India.

70 James Johnstone clarifies this distinction between the two
names interchangeably used by the British officers. 'Besides
Samugudting there are other villages on our side, Sitekima, on
the opposite bank of the Diphoo Panee Gorge, and Tesephima,
on outlying spurs of Samagudting. I say Samagudting, as it
has becomethe common appellation, but correctly speaking it
should be Chumookodima.'

71 The British had by then started manufacturing the
cartridge at Fort William, Calcutta. Amarpal Singh gives
more details of the same in his book, *The Siege of Delhi*. 'In
India, manufacture of the new cartridge for the rifle was
commenced at Fort William, Calcutta, in August 1856, with
quantities of the new rifle arriving in the country the same
month . . . Musketry schools were opened to teach the huge
sepoy army employed by the British East India Company
how to use it.' P. XV.

72 *The Aos in 1891*, Vol. 1, pp. 241–45.

73 *Nagas in the Nineteenth Century*, p. 194.

74 Extracts from the *Narrative of an Expedition into the Naga
Territory of Assam*, Vol. 7, part 1, pp. 445–70.

75 *Statistical Account of the Native state of Manipur* by
R. Brown, 1873.

76 *The Nagas in the Nineteenth Century*, pp. 203–14.

77 For the sake of commerce, order and security, the network of
roads across the hills was already beginning to grow since the
early 1820s. 'In the hills to the west, roads were expected to

facilitate the collection of duties at Garo Markets. The idea that payment of duties would create a social bond between government and subjects surfaces in the correspondence on both the malfunctioning taxation of the Garo markets and the north Cachar violence.' Gunnel, p. 234.

There were many discussions regarding the road from Manipur to Assam via the Naga hills but revenue collection from the Naga hills were the least among them. It veered more towards securing political domination of a vast area of land in between Burma and Assam.

78 As early as 1835, the British, short of demarcating a border, assigned responsibilities to both Manipur and Tularam to occupy the Naga Hills. 'When in 1835 our hill villages in North Cachar were found to be constantly suffering from Naga exactions and raids, the Government conceived that the duty of controlling the hostile Nagas devolved jointly upon Tularam and the Manipur state, as the two powers holding jurisdiction over at least some portion of the Naga Hills. it was proposed, therefore, that a line of posts to protect our subjects should be established by Tularam and the Manipuris at Semkhor and along the neighbouring Naga frontier. Tularam protested earnestly that he had no control over the Nagas or any means of checking their raids; while Manipur, whose only system of control consisted in raids as savage as those of the Nagas themselves, did occupy Semkhor for a time and harass the Nagas in a desultory way, the only effect of which was to bring down the hillmen upon our villages in force as soon as the Manipuris had withdrawn.' Page 103, Alexander Mackenzie, *History of the Relations of the Government with the Hill tribes of the North-East Frontier of Bengal.*

79 A more peaceful approach was adopted. Butler induced the Village chiefs to come and meet him. Communication with them opened, although the raids never did stop with that. The important conclusion, however, was the realisation that only

a permanent and strong outpost in the hills will 'effect any good'. Page 109, Alexander Mackenzie, *History of the Relations of the Government with the Hill tribes of the North-East Frontier of Bengal*.

80 Ibid., p. 109.

81 As quoted on page 181, *Nagas in the Nineteenth Century*, Verrier Elwin.

82 Alexander Mackenzie, *History of the Relations of the Government with the Hill tribes of the North-East Frontier of Bengal*, p. 129, 178.

83 Ibid., pp. 129–133.

84 Dobashi was a position introduced by the British to denote the interpreters used to translate not only the Naga dialects to the British administrators but also as translators of the Naga customs and customary laws. It literally means someone knowing two languages. The qualification was to possess some knowledge of either English or Assamese. They obviously were hired from amongst the natives. Dobashis played an important role during the British forays and also for the British administration over the Naga Hills. When first introduced into the Naga Hills in 1842, they were officially called the 'Residency delegates'.

85 India, Collections to India, Political Dispatches (IOL), L/P &S/6 vol. 88, 1867, no,. 131 of 1866, 'Copy of a dispatch to the Secretary to the Government of Bengal, 7 June 1866', nos. 588–91, Enclosure no. 39, Mackenzie, pp. 116–17.

86 https://morungexpress.com/after-48-years-kutsapo-village-brings-back-remains-its-first-matriculate-darjeeling

87 https://www.hindustantimes.com/india-news/in-kohima-veteran-recalls-ww-ii-battle-on-emotional-return/story-XStVkJ7WiXU2P1wN9k6rcP_amp.html
    https://www.hindustantimes.com/cities/others/japan-collects-samples-of-possible-remains-of-wwii-soldiers-who-died-in-nagaland-101650991437433-amp.html

https://nenow.in/north-east-news/nagaland/from-japan-to-kohima-in-quest-of-the-fallen-wwii-heroes.html

88 https://australianhumanitiesreview.org/wp-content/uploads/2017/06/AHR61_Trefalt.pdf

https://www.nippon.com/en/japan-topics/g02255/

https://www.micronesia.emb-japan.go.jp/files/100475916.pdf

89 William IV instituted the three classes of knights of the order, which (in descending order of rank) are Knight Grand Cross or Dame Grand Cross (GCMG), Knight Commander or Dame Commander (KCMG or DCMG, respectively), and Companion (CMG).

90 https://morungexpress.com/looking-back-in-order-to-look-towards-the-future

https://www.eastmojo.com/news/2019/04/04/battle-of-kohima-anniversary-nagaland-renews-bond-with-uk-japan/

https://www.in.emb-japan.go.jp/itpr_en/00_000849.html

https://www.usiofindia.org/events-details/commemoration-75th-anniversary-of-the-battle-of-kohima-and-imphal.html#:~:text=The%20Commemoration%20Ceremony%2C%20on%2004,%2C%20VSM%2C%20GOC%203%20Corps.

https://kohimaeducationaltrust.net/news-and-events/news/kohima-75th-anniversary

91 https://www.hindustantimes.com/india-news/in-kohima-veteran-recalls-ww-ii-battle-on-emotional-return/story-XStVkJ7WiXU2P1wN9k6rcP_amp.html

92 *Kohima*, Arthur Swinson, p. 304.

93 'Columns circled the right flank of the Japanese main position and took Kharasom, a nodal centre of enemy supply tracks, about twenty-five miles due east of Kohima, against considerable opposition. The action of these columns achieved a threefold success. They cut the main northern Japanese supply route at the most awkward time for him,

they constituted a threat to his rear whose strength he found
it difficult to assess, and they stimulated the active support
of the local tribesmen. These were the gallant Nagas whose
loyalty, even in the most depressing times of the invasion,
had never faltered. Despite floggings, torture, execution, and
the burning of their villages, they refused to aid the Japanese
in any way or to betray our troops. Their active help to us
was beyond value or praise. Under the leadership of devoted
British political officers, some of the finest types of the Indian
Civil Service, in whom they had complete confidence, they
guided our columns, collected information, ambushed enemy
patrols, carried our supplies, and brought in our wounded
under the heaviest fire—and then, being the gentlemen they
were, often refused all payment. Many a British and Indian
soldier owes his life to the naked, head-hunting Naga, and
no soldier of the Fourteenth Army who met them will ever
think of them but with admiration and affection. It was clear
now, at the beginning of June, that on the Kohima front the
enemy was breaking and pulling out as best he could. While
he still fought stubbornly as an individual, the cohesion of his
units and the direction of his forces were obviously failing. The
time had come to press on and destroy what was left of the
31st Japanese Division. The Supreme Commander, on the
8th June, issued a Directive that the Kohima–Imphal road
was to be opened not later than mid-July, and I was grateful
to him for not being stampeded by more nervous people into
setting too early a date. I intended that the road should be
open well before mid-July, but I was now more interested
in destroying Japanese divisions than in "relieving" Imphal.'
P. 448, *Defeat into Victory*, Field Marshall Viscount Slim, First
Cooper Square Press Edition, 2000.

94 'In the end, the aborted attack on Dimapur may rank as the
greatest missed opportunity in Japan's invasion of India.'
Daniel Webster in his book *The Burma War*, p. 257.

95 Could Sato have won the battle of Kohima had his anticipation, his grasp, his tactical skill been greater? The answer must be surely, that if he had been allowed to send a regiment to Dimapur, with orders to seize the base and cut the railway, he might well have done. Why did Kawabe order him back? Slim has said that: 'The fundamental fault in their [the Japanese generals'] generalship was a lack of moral, as distinct from physical, courage. They were not prepared to admit that their plans had misfired and needed recasting.' This is undoubtedly true; but at the end of March 1944, Mutaguchi's plans hadn't misfired; they had gone miraculously well, and both he and Sato wanted to exploit their swift success. It was Kawabe whose mental rigidity stopped them; to him, the campaign had to be fought exactly as planned, come failure, or success. Such rigidity is surprising in a general as experienced in action as Kawabe and there was obviously a good reason for his decision. Barker has suggested that this was simply his strict interpretation of the Tokyo directive, which was that 'the strategic areas near Imphal and in North-East India' did not include Dimapur. General Matsutani, however, after his research in the archives of the Imperial Defence College, has pointed out that in all the initial studies for the operation it was anticipated that 31st Division would seize Kohima, then at once despatch a third of its strength, a regimental group, to Imphal. This fact may have unconsciously coloured Kawabe's interpretation of the order; for obviously if a regiment became engaged at Dimapur, forty miles to the north of Kohima, it would be difficult to extract it and despatch it to Imphal as required. In the event, this earlier plan was modified and the whole 31st Division unreservedly committed to Kohima; but it probably remained like a palimpsest on Kawabe's mind. While dealing with this subject, there is the curious story related by Takahide Hasegawa, according to which Colonel Kato represented his divisional commander at a conference with Kawabe and

Mutaguchi, when the precise role of the 31st Division was being thrashed out in December 1943. The dialogue went like this:

MUTAGUCHI: Tell me, Colonel Kato, what is your commander's plan, once he has captured Kohima?

KATO: TO hold it with his main body, to stop any movement through to Imphal, then to send a regiment to Dimapur.

MUTAGUCHI: That's foolish! Why should you stay at Kohima? The enemy will be running back to Dimapur. Your job is to get after them.

According to Hasegawa, 'Kawabe remained silent during this conversation, though he did not approve of all Mutaguchi's ideas.' It may well be that Kawabe did not wish to oppose Mutaguchi on this point immediately but noted his views with the intention of stopping any Dimapur adventure, should it be mooted once the offensive was launched. As already indicated, in Kawabe's rigid conception Imphal remained the main objective, and other objectives had to be judged solely in their relation to it. Pp. 316–18, *Kohima*, Arthur Swinson.

96 Along with the above debate within the Japanese generals, Slim's review of the fragile position of the British forces in Kohima adds some potential possibility to the debate. 'A decade after the events in question Slim wrote that within a week (author's italics) of the Japanese offensive . . . it became clear that the situation in the Kohima area was likely to be even more dangerous than that at Imphal. Not only were the enemy columns closing in on Kohima at much greater speed than I had expected, but they were obviously in much greater strength. Indeed it was soon evident (author's italics) that the bulk, if not the whole, of the Japanese 31st Division, was driving for Kohima and Dimapur.' (*Defeat into Victory*, p. 305.) This assertion deserves examination. If one takes the start of the Japanese offensive into the Naga Hills as 15 March, Slim seems to be saying he was aware by 23 March that the Japanese were in much greater strength than

a regiment. Colonel Hugh Richards wrote that he only became aware of the size of the approaching Japanese force from Naga scouts on 27 March. The 11 Army Group Commander, General Sir George Giffard, wrote in his official dispatch that 'we became aware' that a division was on the way on 29 March. Slim may have been mistaken in his recollection. It is hard to imagine the defenders of the Kohima area would have been left in ignorance of the size of the attacking force if 14th Army had known earlier.' P. 213, *Road of Bones*, Keane.

97 Don Moser, *China, Burma, India (World War II) Alexandria*, Time-Life Books, 1978, p. 156.

98 Mutaguchi could not claim ignorance of the situation. Sato and his fellow commanders all complained about the supply situation before the offensive began. The 31st Division commander recalled that they 'expressed huge concern and each division offered its opinion . . . and tried to spur the senior staff'. A senior air force officer, Lieutenant General Tazoe, commander of the 5th Air Division, who watched the build-up of allied air strength, and the fly-in of Wingate's Chindits, warned Mutaguchi he was facing a very different enemy. 'The Allied power to bring in transport, troops, guns, tanks, and equipment is beyond anything you have visualised.' The army commander, however, ignored the warnings and put his faith in captured stocks. It had worked before in China and Malaya, why not in India? He clearly preferred not to think about what had just happened in the Arakan, or to dwell upon the disastrous experience of the Japanese in New Guinea in 1942, where some troops had resorted to cannibalism when supplies failed to reach them. To bolster his supplies, Mutaguchi looked to the example of Genghis Khan who fed his Golden Horde with cattle on the hoof. Orders were sent out to conduct an experiment to find out how far cattle could march in a day. Some cows were duly selected and taken on a daylong forced march. The beasts managed thirteen kilometres. What Mutaguchi had failed to take into account—or had decided

to ignore—was that the cattle had been marched along roads in the Burmese staging areas and not up steep mountains like those on the Indian frontier. And they had only been tested on their endurance over a day's march, whereas they would be expected to keep moving for nearly three weeks to pass through the Naga Hills. Fifteen thousand cattle were assembled. Mutaguchi also ordered that each division be given ten thousand sheep and goats. The divisional supply officers were less sanguine about the prospect of living off the land. Lieutenant Masao Hirakubo was a supply officer with the 58th Regiment and arrived in Rangoon to a bleak message from the divisional accountant. 'He said to me: "We know this campaign cannot be carried out but GHQ ordered us and we should do this. That is a soldier's destiny. I cannot expect to see you again."' With this gloomy forecast, Hirakubo learned that he was responsible for feeding a thousand men. He remembered back to the arguments he had had with his father in the lead-up to the war. Hirakubo senior had opposed the conflict and told his son that Japan would survive only by building up her trade. 'I was very young and militarised. Always I was shouting at him while he spoke of negotiations and compromise. Now I felt that my father was right. Japan had got the politics all wrong.' Pp. 167–68, *Road of Bones*, Fergal Keane.

99 'In August 1943 Mutaguchi held a war game at his headquarters in Maymyo during which he revealed that he planned to send an entire division to block the road to Dimapur. They would do it by seizing the best defensive position along the route: the lightly defended hill town of Kohima. With Kohima under his control, Mutaguchi would be able to march on to Dimapur and capture the biggest supply base in the region. It would doom the defenders of Imphal and devastate Slim's plans to invade northern Burma. In an official recording only to be released three decades after his death, Renya Mutaguchi described his projected invasion of northeastern India as the first step in turning the tide of war in Japan's favour: 'The motivation for

starting this campaign is nothing but winning the Great Far Eastern War.' The Imperial headquarters and the Southern Area Army under Count Terauchi hoped for a battle that would drive the British back from the Indian frontier. Japan would then consolidate a new defensive line and sit out the monsoon. Mutaguchi and his acolytes still hoped, with a chronic absence of appreciation of the global situation, for a favourable turn in the war in Europe that might, in conjunction with a Japanese victory in India, force the British into a separate peace and out of the war with Japan. Mutaguchi's dream of victory was encouraged by the lobbying of Subhas Chandra Bose, leader of the Indian National Army, who assured both Mutaguchi and Prime Minister Hideki Tojo that India would rise in rebellion once his men planted their flag on Indian soil. The 'March on Delhi' was bragged about on Tokyo radio and spread as a rumour by Japanese agents eager to foment instability in the Indian Army. In Defeat into Victory General Slim speculated that the defeat of British power in India was the ultimate aim of the invasion. "Here was the one place where they could stage an offensive that might give them all they hoped," he wrote. "If it succeeded the destruction of the British forces in Burma would be the least of its results. China completely isolated would be driven into a separate peace; India, ripe as they thought for revolt against the British, would fall, a glittering prize into their hands . . . it might indeed, as they proclaimed in exhortations to their troops, change the whole course of the world war." Certainly Mutaguchi indulged himself in "private speculations" and, according to one author, even day dreamed about riding a white horse into Delhi.' Fergal Keane, *Road of Bones*, pp. 133–34.

100 Arthur Swinson, *Kohima*, p. 250.
101 *Defeat into Victory* by William Slim.
102 Fergal Keane, *Road of Bones*, p. 163.
103 'However, whatever the dissensions or grumblings in the ranks, discipline still remained unimpaired and every position

was held to the last man. It was something of a wonder to British officers to learn how few men there were in some positions. The secret was that the Japanese did not fight to their front if they could fight to a flank. This meant that they had to rely on neighbouring bunkers for the protection, that is "to cover them", while they covered their neighbours. This system involved a good deal of training and discipline, and a consistently high standard in the siting of posts; but it did make the maximum use of fire power. British and Indian troops were psychologically incapable of such tactics, each man preferring to fight to his front and remaining responsible for his own protection. Also, of course, though recognizing the need for head cover, the British hated being entombed in bunkers and liked the free use of their weapons, denied by Japanese-type bunkers. But these bunkers did allow the Japanese to bring down mortar fire on their own positions, when under attack, and time and time again drove the British and Indians from them before they could dig in. And in Burma the Jap mortarmen were the counterparts of the German machine-gunners in the First World War.' P. 235, *Kohima*, Swinson.

104 *Road of Bones*, p. 439.
105 Ibid., p. 442.
106 The entire Naga villages in the Naga hills were affected by the fierce fighting between the Japanese and the British. The villages near Kohima where the main battle happened had a harder time due to the shelling, firing and bombing. I quote from an incident mentioned by Arthur Swinson in his book *Kohima* to show the action and why it was not possible under the circumstances to go to the fields or for that matter to carry out normal activities. 'Like everyone else who saw Kohima Ridge for the first time, the Royal Berkshires were utterly appalled by the scene around them. Their giant commanding officer, Wilbur Bickford, said later: "We were

most profoundly shocked by the conditions which prevailed on Garrison Hill . . . The stench of festering corpses—Japanese, British and Indian—was overpowering. There were no sanitary arrangements and stores of ah descriptions were lying about. It was possible to pick up anything from a Tommy-gun to a pair of ladies' shoes, and the place was a veritable paradise for flies." Major John Nettlefield, the gunner, has written in similar vein: "When we first saw Kohima it was beautifully fresh and green—an attractive town perched on the hills . . . Now . . . the place stank. The ground everywhere was ploughed up with shell-fire and human remains lay rotting as the battle raged over them. Flies swarmed everywhere and multiplied with incredible speed. Men retched as they dug in . . . the stink hung in the air and permeated one's clothcs and hair."' Pp. 128–29, *Kohima*, Arthur Swinson.

Khrienuo Ltu, *World War II in Northeast India*, Barkweaver Publications, Norway, 2019, pp. 166–67.

107 'In at least one infantry brigade there was a sliding scale of rewards for enemy taken dead or alive by the Nagas. Operational Instruction No. 10 for 23 Infantry Brigade (Chindits) ordered payments as follows: Capture alive Japanese officer: Rs 1000 Captured other rank: Rs 500 Dead Jap officer: Rs100 Dead other ranks: Rs 50 Live hostile individual other than Jap: Rs 75 Dead individual other than Jap: Rs 25 . . . In a frank statement of military priorities, the family of a Naga killed in action would be paid just 300 rupees, less than a third of what was paid for a live Japanese officer, whose worth as an intelligence asset was highly valued.' P. 313, Keane, *Road of Bones*.

108 'The sprawling railhead base that had been hacked out of the jungle at Dimapur, a hundred and thirty miles north of Imphal, was similarly laid out and manned. As long as our intentions remained offensive and those of the Japanese defensive, Imphal and Dimapur were suitably organized;

should the roles be reversed, these widespread bases would become a terrible embarrassment. Our whole situation on this Central front had another grave tactical disadvantage. Our only line of communication was the road our engineers had so magnificently built from railhead at Dimapur up the hill to Kohima, and on to Imphal.' P. 382, Slim.

'If the Japanese could take Dimapur and cut the railway there, they could isolate both the valuable oil fields and the airfields serving the American airlift to China, all based in northern Assam. More to the point, here would be their first toe-hold on the plains of India.' *The Battle at Sangshak*, Harry Seaman, Leo Cooper, 1989, page 417.

109 'Within a week of the start of the Japanese offensive, while the 17th Division was still fighting its way out, it became clear that the situation in the Kohima area was likely to be even more dangerous than that at Imphal. Not only were enemy columns closing in on Kohima at much greater speed than I had expected, but they were obviously in much greater strength. Indeed it was soon evident that the bulk, if not the whole, of the Japanese 31st Division was driving for Kohima and Dimapur. I had been confident that the most the enemy could bring and maintain through such country would be one regimental group, the equivalent of a British brigade group. In that, I had badly underestimated the Japanese capacity for large-scale, long-range infiltration, and for their readiness to accept odds in a gamble on supply. This misappreciation was the second great mistake I made in the Imphal battle. It was an error that was likely to cost us dear. We were not prepared for so heavy a thrust; Kohima with its rather scratch garrison and, what was worse, Dimapur with no garrison at all, were in deadly peril. The loss of Kohima we could endure, but that of Dimapur, our only base and railhead, would have been crippling to an almost fatal degree. It would have pushed into the far distance our hopes of relieving Imphal, laid bare to the

enemy, the Brahmaputra Valley with its string of airfields, cut off Stilwell's Ledo Chinese, and stopped all supply to China. As I contemplated the chain of disasters that I had invited, my heart sank. However, I have always believed that a motto for generals must be 'No regrets', no crying over split milk. The vital need was now to bring in reinforcements, not only to replace the vanished reserve in Imphal but, above all, to ensure that Dimapur was held. To achieve this I bent all my energies.' Pp. 404–405.

110   In general, the situation looked so promising that Mutaguchi permitted himself a few moments of his 'private speculations'. Interpreting the intelligence reports which came flooding in from Assam, he suddenly realized that there was a ripe plum ready for picking: the base of Dimapur. This had not figured largely in the initial planning of the campaign, the generals probably assuming that it would be heavily defended; but now it was at his mercy. If Sato took it, which he should be able to do with a regimental group, the British could neither reinforce their beleaguered troops in Kohima and the Imphal Plain, nor use the railway to retreat to India. The whole central front would be paralysed, then smashed. Mutaguchi sent off two signals, the first to Sato ordering him to advance on Dimapur at once, cut the railway, and secure food and supplies for his troops; and the second to General Kawabe, commander of the Southern Area Army, asking him to signal Count Terauchi to request the air cover to Dimapur. Once this request had been agreed, so Mutaguchi calculated, Sato could reach Dimapur in three days. But it was not agreed; Kawabe replied immediately that 'Dimapur is not within the strategic objectives of the 15th Army'. Mutaguchi protested, giving his own interpretation of the order, but Kawabe remained adamant. The reason for the difference in interpretation was this. The Japanese generals had argued so bitterly among themselves during 1943 that the final orders for the Burma

offensive were something of a compromise. The instructions sent to Kawabe by Imperial Army in Headquarters on the 7th January 1944 ran as follows: 'C.-in-C. Southern Army will break the enemy on his front at the opportune time, and will capture and secure the strategic areas near Imphal and in North-East India for the defence of Burma.' But what were 'the strategic areas' and how far did they extend? The phrase was a vague one, capable of many interpretations; Kawabe interpreted it strictly, and Mutaguchi more liberally, stretching it to accommodate his daydreams. Mutaguchi was right, there could be no doubt whatsoever; this was what Napoleon called 'the favourable moment', and Sato had only to hold Dimapur for a month to bring the British to the brink of disaster. But Mutaguchi dared not disobey Kawabe; and the moment passed. Sato's troops were called back, to join in the fight for Kohima. P. 81, *Kohima*, Swinson.

111 If Bokajan didn't impress the 5th Brigade favourably, Dimapur was even worse. The staff captain of the 5th Brigade wrote in his diary: 'The whole place is in one big flap. The L. of C. area are digging and wiring themselves in their offices, and gangs of pioneers are putting slit trenches round the Rest Camp. Transport with wild-eyed Indian drivers is speeding north along the Bokajan road with barely six inches between trucks. Haggard-looking coolies stagger on with loads and the number of refugees gets bigger every hour. They walk slowly along with their whole world on their heads; occasionally one collapses by the road and the others group round, blocking the traffic but doing nothing. Am told there are 80,000 men in this place, but only 10,000 rifles. Can quite believe it. Have never seen so many troops walking around unarmed.' P. 64, *Kohima*, Swinson.

An Army Quarterly article by Stephen Laing described Dimapur and its Manipur Road railway station as they were in 1949: 'Manipur Road, little red brick station, the yards of which were deserted and littered with broken vehicles, ordnance crates, telegraph poles. There were no workshops, ordnance or supply depots, nor were there any military police. Wild elephants, monkeys in quantity, wild pigs and barking deer occupied the old ammunition depot. There was no Adjutant, no Quartermaster's store, no barber, no tailor, no shoemaker, no tanks or lorries, no mules, only two little Nagas driving cattle. The phallic monoliths still stood, and the brick tanks and buildings of the Cachari Kings of Assam.' John Colvin, *Not Ordinary Men*, p. 111.

112 On the 2nd April an officer and his batman, just arrived with 5th Brigade, rode their motorbike into a large canteen issue depot. Walking up to the counter, they found themselves gazing at vast quantities of chocolate, food, toilet requisites, cigarettes, beer, and even whisky. There was not a soul to be seen and their shouts to be served failed to bring anyone. The whole stock was at their disposal. Debating for a moment what might be the most useful stores to take to war, they decided on chocolate, cigarettes, tinned pineapple, and a bottle of whisky, which were all stowed into the saddle bags. The officer then wrote his name and unit on the counter and offered to pay if a bill were sent him. Needless to say, it never was. P. 65, *Kohima*, Swinson.

113 According to oral narratives collected by Reverend Savito Nagi in his book *Reminiscing the Battle of Kohima 1944* the British Army had issued certain monetary rewards for the Nagas.

114 Arthur Swinson quotes the Japanese Captain Tsuneo Sanukawae of the nth Company. 'In the afternoon, the 58th Regiment got ready to attack Kohima from the east. Apparently, unknown to the garrison, its advance guard had entered Naga Village the previous night. Captain Tsuneo Sanukawae of the nth Company has written: "We entered Naga Village at 4 a.m. on the 5th. The town was fast asleep.

After dealing with the sentries we occupied seven depots and took about thirty trucks. The enemy had not noticed our advance and at 9 a.m. came to the depots to draw their rations. We got them and made them prisoner. At 10 a.m. I was prepared to attack the town, but at that moment we were fired on by artillery. At 1300 hours we informed our main body that we had occupied Kohima Village, and an hour later they arrived. We could not say we had won Kohima until we had gained the hill beyond the road junction, so we attacked . . . Praying to God, we rushed into action, under cover of light machine-gun fire, throwing grenades as we went. Naoje Koboyashi, another member of the Company, has written in similar vein: 'When we reached Kohima we were all tired out after the ceaseless advance day and night, and the troops fell asleep where they were. At first light I looked across towards the Hill [i.e. Garrison Hill] and could see the enemy soldiers walking about . . . they still seemed not to realize we were there." At this point it may be worth mentioning that the 58th Regiment was the crack formation of the Division, with a proud tradition and a long series of victories behind it. The Regimental depot was at Echigo, in the Niigato Prefecture, 150 miles north of Tokyo, on the west coast. This is an area famous for its rice harvest, and most of the men were of farming stock. They were, therefore, tough, self-reliant, and accustomed to hardship. Most of them had seven or eight years service behind them. The 58th considered themselves superior to the 13 8th, and had no great opinion of the 124th at all. However, they had been somewhat shaken by the action at Sangshak and by the ferocious defence put up by Hope-Thompson's brigade. Many good officers and N.C.O.s had gone down leading attacks, and the Regiment arrived at Kohima somewhat mauled, and temporarily exhausted. However, its fighting spirit and morale still remained unimpaired; and in a matter of hours it was launched into the attack.' Pp. 73–74, *Kohima*, Swinson.

115 Besides the trust reposed in him by the Nagas, the author had a certain fascination for him as he was a classmate of the popular British novelist Graham Greene.

116 'Richards was now very much occupied with administrative problems. The Japanese had cut the water supply on G.P.T. Ridge and only a trickle was coming through the pipe. Orders had therefore to be issued, rationing each man to a pint a day, a pitiable amount in the warm climate, and in the heat of battle. Fighting is the most dehydrating occupation known to man. Lieut.-Colonel Borrowman, now Richards's second-in-command, worked hard at the administrative arrangements, as did Major Franklin, second-in-command of the Royal West Kents. A large number of chagals (canvas water containers) were available, and using these, and anything else they could improvise, the troops showed great ingenuity in dodging snipers and mortar fire, to brew up "char". The constant shelling and mortaring, however, was ripping the leaves off the branches and the branches off the trees, so that each day the position became more exposed. Even the luxuriant growth of rhododendrons surrounding the D.C.'s bungalow and the Club area was ravaged, though some hardy bushes blossomed unconcerned. The sniping grew so bad that all movement in the daytime in the neighbourhood of Richards's headquarters became extremely hazardous. His wireless set had failed on the morning of the 5th, as the batteries were exhausted and his charging engine had not arrived. He mentioned the matter to Laverty, to be told that the Royal West Kents' engine had all it could do recharging their own batteries. So Richards was now cut off from the outside world, and all signals from Warren or anyone else had to go to Laverty. The number of walking wounded was beginning to mount up; and Colonel Young considered that, as they'd been able to walk in, they should be able to walk out. So a party was organized, the guide being Lieutenant Corlett (the Assam Regiment subaltern who had taken the

withdrawal message through to Jessami), helped by a Naga detailed by Charles Pawsey. The commander of the party was Major Franklin, and a platoon of the 4th/7th Rajputana Rifles, from the company just arrived, acted as escort. When evening came, and there was a lull in the fighting, the party, which now totalled some 100 wounded, plus some non-combatants, slipped out of the perimeter by I.G.H. Spur with the escort, and made its way down the precipitous slopes into the Zubza nala. The risks were great, as everyone knew, and if they bumped anything but a small patrol they'd be lucky to survive the journey. However, all went well; no Japs were encountered and for once the guides didn't lose the way. By daylight the party were safe in Zubza, without a wound.' Pp. 84–85, *Kohima*, Swinson.

117 'World War II in Northeast India: A Study of Imphal and Kohima Battles' is the doctoral thesis of Khrienuo Ltu, p. 166.

118 Ibid., p. 131.

119 Swinson, *Kohima*, pp. 7–8.

120 Ibid., p. 10.

121 Ibid., p. 12.

122 Ibid., p. 28.

123 Ltu, p. 172.

124 *Kohima 1944 Battle Story*, Chris Brown, p. 90.

125 'As has been said, the "conquest" of India via Imphal had become the obsession of General Mutaguchi, Commander of the Japanese 15th Army. Mutaguchi believed that if Imphal, capital of India's Manipur State, situated in a long high plain in the jungle-covered Naga and Chin Hills, could be captured, the opportunity would be provided for the Japanese-raised Indian National Army under their Bengali leader, Subhas Chandra Bose, to light a fire of revolution which would render India impotent as a base against Japan. Britain might be neutralized, the United States isolated and Japanese forces carried to a junction with Germany in the Middle East.

Although Tojo, who was both Prime Minister and Minister of War, believed that "our main objective lies in India", others, including Mutaguchi's Divisional Commanders, and the Commander, Burma Area Army, Lieutenant-General Kawabe, said that there must be "no mad rush into Assam". Nevertheless, the original concept of a new defence line to defeat a British return to Burma had been superseded, at least in Mutaguchi's mind, in favour of his own ambitions. In particular, instead of authorizing only four battalions of 31 Division to attack Kohima, he had decided to employ the whole division to block British supply to Imphal and then move to India through Dimapur. It should be noted, however, that under interrogation after the war, General Miyazaki, commanding 31 Division Infantry Group during the Kohima battle, said that the task assigned to 31 Division was only "to occupy Kohima in order to cut off the retreat of the Allied troops in Imphal". Whatever Mutaguchi intended, the Japanese Higher Command may not have seriously contemplated an invasion of India by land in 1944, only such a serious defeat of Anglo-Indian forces that Subhas Chandra Bose would be able to lead his Indian National Army into India and thus achieve a virtually bloodless conquest. It might have happened had the Japanese not lost in the Arakan, had the Chindits failed, had 5th and 7th Indian and 2nd British Divisions been kept from the battle, had the British not held at Kohima, and had the Japanese not failed to provide for adequate air power, supply, transport and artillery, or to grasp the training, drive and morale of the new XIV Army. But, as we saw in Chapter II, the Second Arakan operation had been started too early by the Japanese and its value as a distraction from Imphal had been vitiated by Mountbatten's brilliant procurement of the enormous quantity of transport aircraft needed for the rediversion of 5th and 7th Divisions to Imphal. The Japanese were not only beaten in Arakan, but

British IV and XXXIII Corps had time to prepare the ground
in the Imphal area to the north-east, while the Japanese
15 Division ("Ball of Fire")a was still below strength. Without
Kohima, it would have been a damned close-run thing. For
its part, the British command incorrectly supposed that, since
the terrain towards the Chindwin across which the Japanese
would advance was so impenetrable, the latter would attack
Kohima in regimental strength only. This assumption was
strengthened by the British belief that the main Japanese
target was Dimapur, with its vast go-downs and railhead.
In fact, although General Sato's orders were only to take
and hold Kohima, his 31 Division did attack in divisional
strength. His task was made easier by a secondary British
road from Humine to Kohima recently "opened" by General
Ouvry Roberts, commanding 23rd Division. It was reasonable
therefore for the British to suppose that 31st Division would
reduce its efforts at Kohima in favour of Dimapur, if not that
the 4th Battalion Queen's Own Royal West Kents would
hold as long as they did. In the end the Japanese did not
reduce their efforts, but the Royal West Kents did hold out.'
    Pp. 42–44, *Not Ordinary Men*, John Colvin.
126 *Road of Bones*, Fergal Keane, p. 314.
127 'Even before the next phase began, of extermination, the
    Japanese had lost 30,000 dead and 23,000 seriously wounded
    out of 84,000. Still today there are letters, even articles in the
    Tokyo press about Kohima, but Japanese do not talk willingly
    of "that great bitter battle".' *Not Ordinary Men*, p. 302.
128 'The plight of the wounded has been touched on before,
    especially with reference to 4th Brigade. Though there was
    a good deal of rain before they finished their 'hook' and
    attacked G.P.T. Ridge, conditions then were nothing like
    as bad as they became later on, when the rain poured down
    steadily, day after day. By then 4th Brigade and 6th Brigade
    fortunately had a firm link to the road, but 5th Brigade, up in

Naga Village, still had to rely on the Nagas and the precipitous trail across the Zubza valley. Of the situation in mid-May, the staff captain wrote: ". . . having been patched up at the A.D.S., the wounded must endure the nightmare three-hour journey down the precipitous slope into the nala, and across it, and up on to the road. This, on a swaying stretcher carried by four faithful Nagas, often as not under mortar fire. Then a forty-three-mile trip by ambulance down the tortuous road into the torrid heat of Dimapur. Then later on a two-day journey by train to Shillong or Chittagong. Then God knows what. Am continually amazed at the patience of the troops; they he still beneath the blankets, white with pain, but uncomplaining. It's a miracle that so many survive." The trail across the Zubza valley, it should be noted, was not only used to bring wounded down, but to take supplies up. Usually trouble was taken to see that the two columns didn't meet, but on at least one occasion they did. The track at this point was narrow, and flanked on one side by a cliff face and the other by the khud. Understandably the doctor leading the wounded column wanted the mules to go back but that was impossible, the track being too narrow for them to turn. The only solution, therefore, was to ask the Pathans to edge their mules against the cliff face, and hope they'd stay docile, without lashing out with their hind legs; then to see if the Nagas could squeeze past them. As there were about seventy mules, this meant that each wounded man had seventy chances of being kicked to his death, which rather lengthened the odds against the whole party surviving. However, the Pathans spoke gently to their charges in a language they understood, and slowly the column quietened down. Then, at a signal from the column commander, the grinning Nagas eased forward with the first stretcher, gripped the cliff edge with their toes, and shuffled happily along it. Then the next party came . . . and the next. Within half an hour all the wounded were past the mule column and on their way towards the nala. At Kohima this kind of crisis and improvisation occurred almost daily in the business of evacuating wounded; and every time, the Nagas did what was demanded of them. How many lives were owed to the courage and skill of these remarkable hillmen will never be known; but the figure must certainly run into thousands. A vivid and accurate description of the life of an ordinary Jock in the 5th Brigade box, up at Naga Village, was written, while still in action, by Major W. B. Graham, of the Camerons. He is awakened by a shake, while it is still dark. He is fully clothed, and probably has been for weeks. He does not sit up because the roof of the fox-hole is only two feet from the floor. Instead, he slides forward to his stand-to post, where the floor has been deepened. The other two or three occupants of the fox-hole are doing the same thing, pushing aside the slightly sodden blankets they have been sharing. One is already awake, as he was the last on "stag" or sentry. If possible, there should never be fewer than four in a fox-hole, or stag comes round too often. Even with four it comes round twice in a night, as it is forbidden to do more than one hour consecutively. Equipment on, rifle or automatic in the hand, grenades ready, all are now staring out into the blackness . . . In fifteen minutes it will be first light . . . and fifteen minutes after that it will be stand-down, that is, unless the mist fails to clear. But all being well, they can mount a single sentry at, say quarter past five, and the day has started. No one, however, gets out of his fox-hole, though it may be cramped and hurriedly dug. Fox-holes are all inter-supporting and integral parts of a defensive position, but in a way they are independent units. There should be no movement between them by night, and as little as possible by day. One man may have to crawl outside to perch over the hole dug to meet the needs of nature. Another will be preparing the morning "brew" with the aid of a Tommy-cooker, a tin with petrol or meth, as fuel. It is the only method of cooking allowed when in contact with the enemy. The arrival of the ration columns, whether by coolie, mule, motor transport, or plane, is the main event of the day, not only because the actual rations are so important, but because along with them comes the mail, the rum issue, and Seac, the Army newspaper. Mail is received like manna, for it is the only link with another world . . . In the early morning, however, the arrival of the rations is in the vague future. The first business of the day is to get organized. Then, if there is nothing doing, rest. Always rest—at any moment it may cease to be possible . . .' Pp. 223–25, *Kohima*.

129 Slim, *Defeat into Victory*, pp. 386–87.

130 'At this juncture there is no doubt that without the determined actions of the crews and ground staffs of the RAF and USAAF the battles of Imphal and Kohima would have been lost, and Dimapur would have fallen. From 27 March onwards, the troops at Imphal and Kohima relied on the tireless determination of the pilots and ground crew with their Dakotas. Later, Mountbatten, who as Supreme Commander of SEAC had his own private Dakota, said that if one piece of equipment more than any other could be said to have won the Burma War, it was the Dakota. The crisis at Imphal and Kohima, eased by the arrival of 5th Indian Division, continued into April, but by then Slim began to feel more confident because, under the wings of the air forces, reinforcements were flowing in. The RAF had been active in preparing for the showdown at Imphal. The Headquarters of 221 Group RAF under Air Vice Marshal Vincent was established beside the main airstrip at Imphal. This and Palel were all-weather strips, supported by fair weather strips at Kangla, Tulihal, Wanjing and Sapam. These airstrips relied on interlocking ground cover material called Meccano, and on Bithess, a hessian strip covered by

bitumen, which worked well until the main monsoon rains started. In 1943 the RAF had set up radar posts and observer units well forward of Imphal towards the Chindwin valley. One very important observation point and radar station had been established near Tamu in 20th Division's area. This was connected by land line to headquarters, and gave advanced warning of any attacking aircraft. The land line link was vital because radar and radio communication was so unreliable in such mountainous country. The withdrawal from Tamu by 20th Division (4 March–1 April) created severe problems for the RAF which thereby lost one of its most valuable warning systems, just at a time when the Japanese were developing the technique of low-flying attacks by just a few aircraft in order to avoid detection. During the weeks before the battle actually started, the RAF had set up an impressive defensive system, but the Japanese with their Sally bombers and Oscar fighters had made a number of damaging attacks, since the Oscars were able to outmanoeuvre the Hurricanes. The tables began to turn in November 1943 when squadrons of Mk 8 Spitfires flew in to the base. During the next three months, Spitfires destroyed or damaged more than 100 Japanese aircraft for the loss of five pilots. At the same time, American Mustangs and Lightnings attacked forward Japanese airfields which had ineffective warning systems, destroying more than 100 aircraft on the ground, and forcing the Japanese to withdraw their aircraft to bases more than 500 miles away near Rangoon.' P. 74.

131 'The Japanese had no transport aircraft and few mechanical vehicles by this time. Instead, they mobilized the animal power of north Burma and the hills on a scale unprecedented since the time of the old Burmese kings. They also brought their own horses. In Operation Imphal 12,000 horses and mules, 30,000 oxen and more than 1,000 elephants crossed the Chindwin. The scale of animal fatality was colossal.

During the campaign Japanese horses survived only fifty-five days on average and mules seventy-three days. All the horses and mules had died by August and the cattle had also perished or been eaten. Only the elephants survived.' P. 382, Bayley and Harper, *Forgotten Armies*.

132 https://kohimaeducationaltrust.net/resource-material/documents/nagas-role-in-world-war-ii.pdf

133 The Naga Army under A.Z. Phizo gave him the title of General.

Scan QR code to access the
Penguin Random House India website